The Necessity of God

Ontological Claims Revisited

The Necessity of God

R. T. Allen

Transaction Publishers
New Brunswick (U.S.A.) and London (U.K.)

Copyright © 2008 by Transaction Publishers, New Brunswick, New Jersey.

All rights reserved under International and Pan-American Copyright Conventions. No part of this book may be reproduced or transmitted in any form or by any means, electronic or mechanical, including photocopy, recording, or any information storage and retrieval system, without prior permission in writing from the publisher. All inquiries should be addressed to Transaction Publishers, Rutgers—The State University of New Jersey, 35 Berrue Circle, Piscataway, New Jersey 08854-8042. www.transactionpub.com

This book is printed on acid-free paper that meets the American National Standard for Permanence of Paper for Printed Library Materials.

Library of Congress Catalog Number: 2008017618
ISBN: 978-1-4128-0832-3
Printed in the United States of America

Library of Congress Cataloging-in-Publication Data
Allen, R. T., 1941-
    The necessity of God : ontological claims revisited / R. T. Allen.
        p. cm.
    Includes bibliographical references and index.
    ISBN 978-1-4128-0832-3
    1. God—Proof. Ontological. I. Title.
BT103.A43   2008
212'1—dc22
                                                                    2008017618

Contents

Preface

Every person acquires a world view, some sort of picture, now matter how vague, of the whole of reality and what sorts of thing exists in it. And within that picture, the existence of some thing or some things will be taken wholly for granted as the background to and support of everything else. Its or their existence will be rarely questioned. The cosmos or universe, the gods, God, Brahman, Heaven, the Absolute—all these and others have been held to be that which necessarily exists and upon which all other beings depend in one way or another. European philosophers from Plato and Aristotle onwards, and later also theologians, have offered arguments, even proofs, to show that their chosen candidates for the role of the necessary being or beings, which support the rest of reality, do actually exist. Those arguments started from some familiar aspect of the world around us and aimed to show that it depended upon something beyond itself. But St. Anselm famously produced a new sort of argument altogether, rather two arguments, to show directly that the ideas of "that than which no greater can be conceived" (the "maximal" being) and of God as the (metaphysically) perfect being, cannot be mere ideas but must be instantiated in reality. In other words, simply by examining these ideas we shall see that the maximal or perfect being or God (the three being taken to coincide) must exist. This form of argument is known as the ontological argument.

In this book I shall set forth what I hold to be the valid core of previous ontological arguments. It does not, nor cannot, prove that God exists but only that something or other necessarily exists. But then, also in an *a priori* manner and without inferring anything from what in fact exists, I proceed to show that that which necessarily exists is one, trans-finite, eternal, personal, and the archetype of personal existence; in short, that it is God as classically conceived. As for everything else that may exist, it must be finite and dependent for its existence upon God as its creator and sustainer. Finally, I argue that a thorough-going use of personal categories for God will remove recent claims that the existence of the finite world makes him also finite in some respects. In almost every other context, I would be the first to reject any such way of thinking, for few things are more erroneous in philosophy and disastrous in practice than abstract and artificial constructions produced out of one's own head and without constant reference to concrete reality. Yet that which necessarily exists may be the one exception.

Before this constructive argument, I examine in Chapter 1 previous examples of ontological arguments in order to show exactly where they go wrong and to extract the valid core which is obscured within them. This will make clear the difference between them and the new version presented in Chapter 2. The reader who is eager to engage with the constructive argument or who feels bogged down in the details of the review of previous ontological arguments would do well to skip Chapter 1 and to return to it later.

1

Previous Ontological Arguments
for the Existence of God

1. Introduction

The likely reaction of most people when they first encounter an ontological argument for the existence of God is that it seems to pull a very
big rabbit out of an obviously empty hat. Something must be wrong with
it, but it seems difficult to pin down what it is. Precisely because a new
version will be presented in the next chapter, the previous ones will be
reviewed here in order to ascertain exactly where they do go wrong and
to make clear how the revised version will differ. We shall consider only
those criticisms which apply specifically to these arguments and not those
which attack this whole way of thinking, the principal one of which is
that the idea of necessity cannot apply to things but only to propositions.
Thus, it may be allowed that "X is Y" can be legitimately said to be necessarily true, but one cannot legitimately say that X necessarily exists. I
have nothing to say that has not been said elsewhere about such general
criticisms,[1] except to argue that it is impossible to perceive the world,
to think about it and to act within it, without implicitly applying to it
the categories or modalities of possibility, impossibility, and necessity.
That is, we would suffer complete practical and mental paralysis if we
could not implicitly or explicitly raise and try to answer such questions
as: "What could happen next? Could this change? Could I do that or is
it impossible? Must this always happen? Is it really necessary to do A
in order to achieve B?"

2. St. Anselm's Two Arguments

Because it was the first to be formulated and is commonly taken to
be *the* ontological argument, we shall begin with Anselm's first version

of it.[2] It is that we can form the intelligible idea of "that than which no greater can be conceived" ("the maximal being" as Hartshorne refers to it); that it cannot be thought only as an idea and not to exist in reality; for, if so, it could be conceived also to exist in reality, which would be greater than existing only in the understanding; hence, it must exist in reality as well.

The usual objection to it is that "existence is not predicate" because thinking of something as existing adds nothing to the mere idea of it. This is often taken to be Kant's objection but Hume had already asserted that to "reflect on any thing simply, and to reflect on it as existent, are nothing different from each other. That idea, when conjoin'd with the idea of any object, makes no difference to it."[3] For example, unlike its design, weight, colour, and shape, the existence of one of Kant's thaler coins is not one of its properties. Again, the face in a picture compiled by the police does not look any different when the witness says: "That's him!" that is, when instead of being a picture of a possible person it is recognised as one of an actual person. Therefore "that than which no greater can be conceived," God or Perfection, cannot have existence as one of their properties and, therefore, it is not self-contradictory to claim that they do not exist.

But Hartshorne, and Robert Flint before him, while conceding that existence as such is not a predicate, rightly asserted that the *modality* of existence is.[4] It makes a great deal of difference to how we conceive of something when we place it in another existential modality; once we realise that a perpetual motion machine is impossible, we shall not waste any time by trying to construct one nor in investigating any claim to have invented one. Conversely, if we were to discover that something exists or happens necessarily, then we would give up any intention of removing or preventing it, or any hope or fear that it might disappear or not happen. Again, not having to exist *is* one of the properties of merely possible entities, such as ourselves, and so we take care to protect ourselves.

Moreover, despite having Kant's authority behind it and being endlessly repeated, the claim that existence itself is not a predicate is false. True, it is not exactly the same as all or most other predicates, but the affirmation that something exists does make a difference to our idea of it. As for Hume's argument, that is a paramount example of picture thinking; our ideas, in his and empiricist epistemology generally, are mental pictures. Hence our ideas, as mental images, will not change when we think of that of which they are the images as real or unreal, just as features in the face in the identikit or e-fit picture do not change when the witness exclaims, "That's him!" But it makes a great deal of difference to the police's *idea* of the person portrayed to know that he is real and not just someone imagined; they now have someone to look for, find, and question, whose movements they can hope to track, whose DNA they may be able to find and examine, etc. Similarly, when children learn that Father Christmas does not exist, they cease to write letters to him. Again, if Kant had discovered that he had, after all, a hundred thalers in his pocket, then he would have been able to spend or invest them. Take away the thought of something's existence, and you take away the idea of interaction with it. To affirm that something exists is to affirm that its powers are actualised, and things *are* their powers, or at least what they are includes their powers: money that cannot be spent is not money; women who do not cast spells are not witches; atoms that cannot combine in the ratio of 2:1 with oxygen atoms to form water molecules are not hydrogen atoms.

This general objection is therefore no objection at all. Nevertheless, Anselm's argument is not saved by its removal, as we shall see in a moment. Instead, the fault in Anselm's argument lies elsewhere. In fact, there are two errors in his argument.

The first is Anselm's assumption there is but *one* being other than which nothing greater can be conceived, and so he seeks to show that the one and only maximal being exists, rather than that maximal being is a category or modality which must be instantiated whether by one or a plurality of beings. It arises from conflating "not having any superior" with "being superior to everything else," and thus by omitting the possibility of a plurality of maximal beings, each equal to the others and all superior to everything else. Anselm could answer that one who is greater than all would be greater than one who is merely one of the equally greatest, for he would be limited by his fellow. Descartes, Flint, and Hartshorne could have provided parallel arguments but did not probably because they aimed to prove the existence of God and, therefore, assumed the unity of maximal being instead of seeking to prove it.[5]

Anselm distinguishes "exists in the understanding" from "to understand that the object exists." But the former conflates two distinct mental acts: merely thinking of (imagining) something and thinking of (imagining) it as existing. The content of this latter act is greater than that of the former one. For in it the object is thought of (imagined) as having its powers actualised: when I imagine that I have won several millions in the lottery, I imagine, not just a lot of zeros added to the total in my bank account but also, at least implicitly, the wonderful things which that sum would enable me to do. Hence in imagining that the maximal being exists, we imagine that its powers are actualised, and hence the content of this act is indeed greater—has more to it—than that of the former act of merely thinking of the maximal being. What Anselm needed to show, therefore, was that the content of "understanding [affirming] that the object exists" is *greater again* than that of the content of simply imagining it to exist. Yes, in this third act its powers are affirmed to be actualised and it becomes something that we need to take into account. But does that make the *content* of the idea of "maximal being" yet greater, so that not to affirm its existence would be a contradiction of the very idea? In what way could it be greater still? Surely the answer is by having *additional* powers, or the same powers to a greater degree, than when it is merely imagined as existing. But to affirm the existence of anything is not to *add* powers to it but to hold to be actualised the powers already contained in, or implied by, the idea of it. Hence the maximal being, attributed with such-and-such powers, both when simply thought of and also when imagined as existing, would have the very same powers but actualised when affirmed to exist. (Of course, if it does exist we may, as with anything else, learn that it has more powers than what we had already attributed to it and also possibly less.) It would not cease to be the idea of that than which no greater can be conceived when not affirmed to exist, that is, unless something very special is added to the idea or drawn out from it. And that again will bring us to the valid element in the argument.

In passing we may note that Kant may have had some inkling of this when he said that a hundred real thalers "do not contain the least coin more than a hundred possible ones."[6] This is not the mistake that it is usually thought to be. His error was to interpret "greater" specifically to mean "greater in number," whereas what he should have said is that Anselm's argument entails that real thalers would have additional or greater powers than those merely imagined as existing, for example, that they would have the purchasing power of 110 thalers rather actually become 110 thalers.

In Ch. III of the *Proslogium*, Anselm adds necessary existence to the maximal being, and produces what is, in effect, his second argument. "It is possible," writes Anselm, "to conceive of a being which cannot be conceived not to exist; and this is greater than one which can be conceived not to exist," and the thought that it might not exist is therefore an "irreconcilable contradiction." It would be a self-contradiction to say that a necessary being would not be greater than a merely possible being. But is it a self-contradiction to say that the idea of a necessarily existing maximal being need not have its counterpart in reality? It looks as if Anselm is defining the maximal being into existence and arguing that because necessary existence is part of its definition, as agreed, then it must exist. Why could we not say that RTA is a necessary being and therefore he must exist? Well, for one thing, there is no reason to say that—whereas necessary existence is of the essence of the maximal being, without it the maximal being would be just another being. Only in the case of the maximal being can we go, and indeed *must go*, straight from idea to reality, from conception to affirmation of existence.

The error in *this* argument is that the idea of the maximal being is really redundant. For the maximal being is now *defined* as that which alone exists necessarily, and its exclusive possession of necessary existence is what makes it the maximal being, and nothing else is being asserted of it. Consequently, by "maximal being" Anselm now means "that which, whatever else it may be, alone necessarily exists." Therefore, what the argument proves is that *necessary being* exists and does so necessarily. This looks like the mere tautology that whatever is a necessary being necessarily exists—or that if X is a necessary being, then X necessarily exists. And that is the problem with this and the following versions of the ontological argument: they appear merely to define the maximal or perfect being or God into existence, or to end up with a mere tautology, or to do both.

But the true meaning of "necessary being necessarily exists" is very different and profound; it is that the *category* or *modality* of necessary being is necessarily instantiated and that therefore something (otherwise unspecified) does necessarily exist. That this *something* is singular and not plural is demonstrated, if at all, apart from and before or after the ontological argument itself. In other words, in the first steps of the argument itself "the maximal being" or "the perfect being" or "God" need to be taken as mere as ciphers for "necessary being" as meaning the "category or modality of necessary being" and nothing more, if the argument is to be valid.

We shall now quickly examine the later versions of Anselm's second argument and show that they follow the same basic pattern and appear to oscillate between defining God into existence and proving a mere tautology while hiding the real and valid argument.

3. The Development of Anselm's Second Argument:
Descartes to Ward

In his Fifth *Meditation*, Descartes took up Anselm's second line of thought and argued that the idea of existence cannot be separated from that of God as a supremely perfect being, and so God must exist. Likewise Leibniz argued that God, as supremely perfect, therefore necessarily exists. Robert Flint followed this pattern of argument; the idea of God is that of a perfect being; in turn, that is the idea of a necessarily existing one; and thus, without the affirmation of existence, the idea of God is merely "either the idea of nonentity, or the idea of an idea, and not the idea of a perfect being at all."[7]

Hartshorne's argument is a more detailed version of Descartes' and, likewise, has two parts. The former is Hartshorne's definition of God as (metaphysical) Perfection, which is in terms of his own panenthenism (God in some way containing the world but not being contained by it, depending upon a world but not upon any particular one, and surpassing previous states of himself as well as all other beings). I shall omit that complication and pass to the latter part, the formal proof. I shall now recast it from its symbolical form into English, and include Hartshorne's own accompanying comments in brackets, with my own in square brackets:

Hartshorne's formal proof:

1. "There is a perfect being" entails "It is necessarily true that there is a perfect being." (Perfection could not contingently exist: Anselm's principle.)
2. It is necessarily true that there is a perfect being or it is not necessarily true that there is a perfect being.
3. "It is not necessarily true that there is a perfect being" entails "It is necessarily not true that it is necessarily true that there is a perfect being." (Modal status always necessary: Becker's Postulate [e.g., possible beings cannot become impossible and vice-versa].)
4. From (2) and (3): It is necessarily true that there is a perfect being or it is necessarily not true that it is necessarily true that there is a perfect being.
5. "It is necessarily true that it is not necessarily true that there is a perfect being" entails "it is necessarily true that there is not a perfect being." (From (1).)
6. It is necessarily true that there is a perfect being or it is necessarily not true that there is a perfect being. (From (1), (4), and (5).)
7. It is not necessarily true that there is not a perfect being. (Perfection is not impossible.)

8. It is necessarily true that there is a perfect being. (From (6) and (7).)
9. "It is necessarily true that there is a perfect being' entails 'that there is a perfect being." (Modal axiom.)
10. There is a perfect being. (From (8) and (9).)[8]

Hartshorne thinks that (7) is the hardest to justify, for it needs the support of another theistic proof, that is, to show that God and Perfection are identical. This may possibly betray Hartshorne's own concern over the real import of his argument. Let us pare down the argument to the key element by substituting "a necessary being" for "a perfect being."
Substitution 1:

1. "There is a necessary being" entails "It is necessarily true that there is a necessary being." (Necessity could not contingently exist.)
2. It is necessarily true that there is a necessary being or it is not necessarily true that there is a necessary being.
3. "It is not necessarily true that there is a necessary being" entails "It is necessarily not true that it is necessarily true that there is a necessary being". (Modal status always necessary: Becker's Postulate.)
4. From (2) and (3): It is necessarily true that there is a necessary being or it is necessarily not true that it is necessarily true that there is a necessary being.
5. "It is necessarily true that it is not necessarily true that there is a necessary being" entails "it is necessarily true that there is not a necessary being." (From (1).)
6. It is necessarily true that there is a necessary being or it is necessarily not true that there is a necessary being. (From (1), (4), and (5).)
7. It is not necessarily true that there is not a necessary being. (A necessary being is not impossible.)
8. It is necessarily true that there is a necessary being. (From (6) and (7).)
9. "It is necessarily true that there is a necessary being" entails "that there is a necessary being." (Modal axiom.)
10. There is a necessary being. (From (8) and (9).)

From this substitution we clearly see that Hartshorne's version of the argument does not prove that the maximal being, God or Perfection exists unless "the maximal being," "God," and "Perfection" mean *no more than* "necessary being" or "necessary existence," as suggested above. For it is the modality of necessary being that is the active ingredient in all such proofs. Hence, it is the existence of necessary being (of some sort or other) that it really does prove, no less and no more. Furthermore Hartshorne, like Anselm, merely assumes that necessary existence is Perfection or God, that is, *that no other necessary being can exist* besides God or the one Perfect being.

The final version in this brief review is that formulated by Keith Ward, which I shall now summarise, for convenience, in a more formal manner with my own elucidations in square brackets:

1. (a) The notion of a being which, if it is possible, is actual [that is, of a necessary being], is coherent.
    (b) We do not know (i) if it is necessarily true that there could be no being which could be actual but not simply possible and not actual [that is, we do not know (i) whether it is necessarily true that a necessary being could not be actual].
    (c) Lacking a proof of (i), we have to admit that there could be a being which, if actual, is possible.
    (d) Therefore from (c) that being is actual.
2. (a) Suppose that there is a being greater than any other conceivable being (or a "most perfect [sic] conceivable being").
    (b) One of its properties will be necessary existence, because the most perfect conceivable being it must possess the property of self-existence and so to be incapable of change or destruction against its will.
    (c) What is self-existent must be uncaused.
    (d) From (c), the most perfect conceivable being either exists or is impossible.
    (e) If it can exist, it must, for it cannot be brought into being [by something else] or come into being for no reason at all.
    (f) Therefore it cannot be conceived not to exist.
    (g) Therefore from (1) it does exist.
3. (a) By having limits set by some other being, any limited being depends for its nature on that other being.
    (b) Hence, at best it can be only conditionally necessary.
    (c) An object retaining the same properties when its antecedent conditions vary would be necessary.
    (d) But it would have to be outside the causal nexus of the universe; therefore its nature would follow from itself; and so it would be self-existent [and absolutely necessary].
    (e) From 2 (g) and 3 (b) and (d), there can and must be only one [absolutely] necessary being and that is the perfect being.[9]

Ward's version has the merit (like Descartes') of facing the question of the unity of necessary and perfect being, and also (unlike Descartes) that of an attempt to prove it. It also has the merit of distinguishing necessary from perfect being and of attempting to prove separately that something must instantiate both of them. That is, it first establishes a general principle—that a (that is, any) being which, if possible, is actual, must therefore exist. Then it proceeds to show that the most perfect conceivable being (rather, mode of being, so as not to appear to beg the question of unity) would be a necessarily existing (mode of) being and therefore must exist. It then shows that there can be only one perfect being. This makes it the clearest formulation of the Anselmian tradition so far. Does it succeed? Not quite.

What is argued in stage (1), apart from the qualifications added in (b) and (c), is that the idea of a necessary being is coherent and that therefore such a being exists. Ward also says that the conclusion of stage (1) is that all possible necessary beings actually exist.[10] The problem with these formulations, as we have seen, is not that they wrong in themselves but that they appear to collapse into the mere tautology that if X is a necessary being, then necessarily it exists. Consequently, in stage (2) Ward takes up the idea of maximal or perfect being and, following the tradition, argues that as such it would have to exist necessarily and so must exist. But, as before, this shows only that *something*, as yet to be further specified as perfect in *other* ways, necessarily exists. It is necessary being itself, and not perfection as something additional to it, which is proved to exist. Consequently, stage (3) does not show that there can be only one perfect being, but that there can be only one necessary being. From (2) and (3) it follows that the one necessary being is perfect (if that is a coherent conception) but leaves open what else is entailed by perfection. Hence, the whole argument does not prove what it is assumed to have proved or to have failed to prove.

Ward himself acknowledges its limitations and suggests that Kant's opinion, that the other forms of argument presuppose the ontological one, be reversed and that the ontological argument, "being the most abstract and general of all, presupposes and relies upon all the other forms of argument for God which lie hidden in it."[11] That is, if it is used for an argument to the existence of God or to that of anything more than necessary being itself.

The result of this survey of the Anselmian tradition is that it has hit upon something very important but has produced invalid or incomplete arguments because it encrusts the valid core of those arguments with two assumptions or mere assertions: the unity of necessary being (except in the case of Ward) and the other attributes of that which is shown to be necessary and therefore actual. The valid core, hidden beneath the use "the maximal being" or "the perfect being" or "God," is that *necessary being itself* does exist and so exist necessarily. That is, the *category* or the *modality* of necessary existence is necessarily instantiated. In the next chapter, that valid core will be formally presented without any accretions which would only obscure it.

Notes

1. For example, by Hartshorne in *The Logic of Perfection*, Chs. IV and XIV. For further discussions of ontological arguments for the existence of God, see the books by J. Barnes, J. Hick and A.C. McGill, A. Platinga, and G. Oppy in the Bibliography (the last also reviews ontological arguments other than those claiming to prove the existence of God). See also the other books and articles mentioned in them, and Ward's *Rational Theology and the Creativity of God*. Another important book is F.N. Findlay's *The Ascent to the Absolute*. Findlay rejects the validity of the ontological argument in its usual forms and points to the version to be formulated below in Ch. 2, but uses other arguments (p. 97). He also shows that the logic of reasoning about necessary being must be different from that about merely possible beings.
2. *Proslogion*, Ch. II, in *St Anselm: Basic Writings*.
3. *Treatise of Human Nature*, I ii, 6.
4. R. Flint, *Theism* (1877), quoted in the original Introduction to *St Anselm: Basic Writings*, 45; Hartshorne, *Logic of Perfection*, Ch. VII.
5. Descartes simply stated, rather than simply assumed, that there cannot be two or more Gods conceived as perfect and eternal (*Meditations*, V). And Leibniz, immediately before giving his ontological argument (*Monadology* §45), had used the Principle of Sufficient Reason to argue that all finite things must depend for their existence upon one, perfect and infinite Being, God, who therefore exists. His ontological argument is an addition to, and thus is supplemented by, his cosmological argument and so does not merely assume that necessary existence is unitary. Spinoza, in effect, defined God-or-Nature into existence by his definition of substance as that which exists in itself from which, by omitting and mention of relations, he proved that there can be only one such substance and that everything else is an attribute or mode of it (*Ethics*, Pt I, "Of God").
6. *Critique of Pure Reason*, 505.
7. Descartes, *Meditations*, V; Leibniz, *Monadology* §45; Flint, see above n.4.
8. *Logic of Perfection*, Ch. VI.
9. *Rational Theology and the Creativity of God*, 26-8.
10. ibid., 28.
11. ibid., 29; cf. 48.

2

Something Must Exist

The previous versions of the ontological argument examined in Chapter 1 erred in seeking to prove that the idea of something supposedly further specified—that than which no greater can be conceived, God, metaphysical perfection—cannot be a mere idea but must be instantiated in reality.[1] But the active ingredient in those versions is the modality of necessary being itself, so that what they actually prove is that necessary being necessarily exists, and *not* that the maximal being or perfect being or God exists. But "necessary being necessarily exists" appears to mean the mere tautology that if *X* is a necessary being, then it exists necessarily. Hence it seems that God, etc. are being defined into existence. Yet, "necessary being necessarily exists" has another and profound meaning which the previous ontological arguments have obscured: that the modality of necessary being cannot be an empty modality such that nothing at all in reality instantiates it but that *something*, otherwise wholly unspecified, must instantiate it. That valid core can be formally presented as follows.

We begin with some definitions following Hartshorne, of the three fundamental modalities of existence:

1. An *impossible* being or event *cannot exist* or happen.
2. A *merely possible* being or event *can exist* or happen and *can not-exist* or not-happen.
3. A *necessary* being or event *can exist* or happen and *cannot not-exist* or not-happen.

The question to be asked is, if and how they can each be instantiated in reality, that is, if anything can exist of the relevant sort.

Impossible Being

This category or modality is that of what cannot exist, and therefore *it cannot be instantiated in reality.* If we can demonstrate that the real existence of an object of thought is logically impossible, then we know that any allegedly real examples of it are illusions: we do not have to examine supposed examples of perpetual-motion machines or Euclidian triangles whose internal angles do not add up to 180 degrees to ascertain that there cannot be any or that any such examples are not in reality examples of that sort of thing. Indeed, the phrase "an impossible being" is a misnomer because the conception of whatever it is that turns out to be impossible thereby proves to be an incoherent combination of incompossible conceptions, a "non-thing." It is necessarily the case that the modality of impossible being is empty.

Merely Possible Being

This category or modality is that of what can exist and can not-exist, and therefore *it can be instantiated, and also might not be instantiated.* Obviously it is instantiated, for otherwise we would not be here to think about it. The point is that it is logically and ontologically possible that in fact nothing at all that is merely possible might exist. The modality of merely possible being may or may not be empty, and whether it is or not cannot be determined *a priori.* As for the existence of any particular merely possible being, or species thereof, we need empirical evidence of its or their existence. We need a living example, or the remains of one, to ascertain if egg-laying mammals exist or have existed, or whether there were flying reptiles. It is necessarily the case that the modality of merely possible being can be instantiated and that it may or may not be instantiated.

Necessary Being

We can divide the question about its instantiation into three sub-questions. Is the idea of "necessary being:"

1.   incoherent and incapable of instantiation?
2.   merely possibly instantiated and thus possibly not instantiated?
3.   necessarily instantiated?

Let us take these suggestions in turn:

(1) The idea of necessary being is not incoherent. On the contrary, denial of its coherence is a self-contradiction (it is the self-contradictory contention that a necessary being is an impossible being). Similarly, the claim that everything which does exist is merely possible and not necessary is either: (a) an empirical induction from entities examined to date and, thus, leaves open the possibilities that the idea of a necessary being

may be coherent and that one day we may find a being which necessarily exists; or (b) an *a priori* claim that nothing could possibly exist necessarily, and thus it both implies the self-contradiction that necessary being is impossible and also it re-introduces necessity in contending that it is *necessarily* the case that nothing necessary can exist and that only merely possible beings can. And any attempt to give up these modal categories entails complete mental paralysis. Therefore the idea of necessary being is coherent and the category or modality of necessary being *can be instantiated.*

(2) Therefore necessary being is possible. But is it merely possible, such that there might be no necessary beings at all. If so, then the modality of necessary being would be that of merely possible being *and so not the modality of necessary being at all.*

(3) Necessary being is that which cannot not-exist, *and therefore the category or modality of necessary being is necessarily instantiated.* The idea of necessary being cannot be a mere idea *but something or other must exist that exemplifies it*, and the modality of necessary being cannot be empty.

To sum up these results:

1. The idea of impossible being *must be* a mere idea (rather, an incoherent assembly of incompossible ideas) and *cannot be instantiated* in reality.
2. The idea of merely possible being *may be* a mere idea and not one instantiated at all in reality or it *may also be* instantiated in reality (as in fact it now is).
3. The idea of necessary being *cannot be* a mere idea and it *must also be instantiated* in reality.

It therefore follows that *there is at least one being that cannot not-exist.*

But about that which exists necessarily we know, so far, nothing more; we do not even know if it is one or many, but only that *something or other* necessarily exists.

This, then, is the valid core of the Anselmian tradition of ontological arguments. We can see this by substituting "the modality of necessary being is instantiated" for "there is a perfect being" in Hartshorne's formal proof.

Substitution 2:

1. "The modality of necessary being is instantiated" entails "It is necessarily true that the modality of necessary being is instantiated." (A necessary being cannot be a merely possible one.)

2. It is necessarily true that the modality of necessary being is instantiated or it is not necessarily true that the modality of necessary being is instantiated.

3. "It is not necessarily true that the modality of necessary being is instantiated" entails "It is necessarily not true that it is necessarily true the modality of necessary being is instantiated." (Modal status always necessary: Becker's Postulate.)

4. From (2) and (3): It is necessarily true that the modality of necessary being is instantiated or it is necessarily not true that it is necessarily true that the modality of necessary being is instantiated.

5. "It is necessarily true that it is not necessarily true that the modality of necessary being is instantiated" entails "it is necessarily true that the modality of necessary being is not instantiated." (From (1).)

6. It is necessarily true that the modality of necessary being is instantiated or it is necessarily not true that the modality of necessary being is instantiated. (From (1), (4), and (5).)

7. It is not necessarily true that the modality of necessary being is not instantiated. (It is not impossible that the modality of necessary being is instantiated.)

8. It is necessarily true that the modality of necessary being is instantiated. (From (6) and (7).)

9. "It is necessarily true that the modality of necessary being is instantiated" entails "that the modality of necessary being is instantiated." (Modal axiom.)

10. The modality of necessary being is instantiated. (From (8) and (9).)

This third rewriting removes any suggestions that some particular necessary being is intended, that there can be only one necessary being, or that the result of the proof is one or more of the three tautologies already mentioned. Hartshorne's formal proof reformulated becomes a longer and more complex version of the valid argument. It may also have two advantages: (a) from (1) to (6) it makes it even more explicit that either the modality of necessary being is instantiated or that the very idea of it is nonsense; and (b) because it clearly distinguishes between the necessary truth, or otherwise, of *propositions* about instantiation of necessary being and the necessary existence of *what those propositions assert*, namely, that necessary being can be instantiated and that it must be instantiated.

I know of no substantial objections to this proof, other than those to any reasoning of this sort, those already mentioned and answered, or those which simply insist on applying to necessary being the terms and categories which do apply to merely possible being. Consequently, it has now been demonstrated that the modality or category of necessary being cannot be uninstantiated—necessary being exists and, therefore, at least one necessary being exists. That is all that we have proved so far. We have not proved that God, Perfection, The One, Brahman, the Absolute, or anything else exists necessarily, but only that *something or other* necessarily exists. And, at present, that is all that we know about it. We do not know, for example, if it is one or many, eternal or temporal, material or immaterial, personal or impersonal, let alone how it (or they) is related to all the merely possible beings with which we are familiar. This is where the ontological argument must end; by itself it can do no more.

But it does give the beginnings of an answer to the question, held by Leibniz and Heidegger to be the fundamental question of metaphysics and thus of all philosophy: "Why does something and not nothing at all exist?" Namely, this is because there is at least one being (of which we as yet know nothing more) that cannot not-exist. There never was when it was not, nor ever will be when it will not be, and therefore it could never be the case that nothing at all exists, ever has existed, or ever will exist.

Likewise, it taken us on the first step towards the Absolute, in the generic sense of that term—namely, that whose existence would explain itself and everything else. In this sense the Absolute is an absolute presupposition of all intellectual enquiry. For, short of it, we go from one antecedent cause to another, from one law to another and more general one, from one particular end or purpose to a more inclusive one without ever finding something that logically completes these regresses or progresses. Whatever else the Absolute may be, it must exist necessarily for otherwise something else would be required to explain its existence and thus it would not be the Absolute after all. At the least we know that somewhere and somehow there is at least one possible candidate for that role.

Here, we must say goodbye to the ontological argument, and we must look elsewhere for further guidance as to what that something, or some things, may be. Of the questions that we could now ask, we shall take up that of singularity and plurality: Can there be many necessary beings or but only one? Let us see if we can answer that question purely by ratiocination and without recourse to any empirical evidence.

Note

1. Findlay did suggest something like what will follow—see above, Ch. 1, n. 1; and P. van Inwagen produced a version of it which he encrusted with the notion of possible worlds (*Metaphysics*, 96-7).

3

Further Attributes of Necessary Being

1. One or Many?

As we have seen, those who have proposed ontological arguments have often assumed that necessary being is unitary. Yet, other cosmologies have included a plurality of ultimate beings which, explicitly or implicitly, have been held to exist necessarily. As examples of the latter we may cite the pluralist idealism of McTaggart[1] and the somewhat similar cosmology of the Samkhya school in Hinduism, in both of which reality consists of a society of everlasting spirits and also the cosmology of those who apparently take the universe as necessarily existing along with its basic constituents, such as the types and numbers of elementary particles. Is it possible to decide non-empirically between these options? One possible way would be to start with either singularism or pluralism and to try to show that it proves incoherent, thus demonstrating by its elimination the truth of the other. Let us take that approach and examine pluralism to see if it is coherent or not.

As was also mentioned in the Chapter 1, Ward rejected a plurality of necessary entities with the argument that by having limits set by some other being, any limited being depends for its nature on that other being, and therefore at most it could be only conditionally necessary—that is, it could exist and be what it is only on certain conditions apart from itself and would not be absolutely necessary such that it could not not-exist whatever else might exist or not. But this does not immediately follow, for there is another possibility. Suppose that there are two necessary beings, *A* and *B*. Consequently, *A* exists necessarily and so does *B*. Yet that is not all. For, since they are both necessary, *A* necessarily exists alongside *B*, and *B* necessarily exists alongside *A*. It is impossible that *A* should exist apart from *B*, and *B* from *A*. Their co-existence cannot be a mere possibility but would be a joint necessity, and that would make them the two poles, centres or foci of a necessarily existing and necessarily differentiated system or society. An internal and wholly necessary plurality cannot be ruled out *a priori*.[2]

That apart, Ward's argument assumes that the two or more necessary entities are not wholly independent and do not interact. But what if they were Aristotelian gods each enclosed in its own thinking about thinking? In that case, it seems, they would not not interfere with each other, and nothing in any would depend upon the others. Nevertheless, each would still be limited by the existence of the others, for they all would have to be isolated from each other and confined wholly within themselves precisely in order not to interact with each other, as are patients in isolation wards. So far, Ward's argument needs a little expansion but its conclusion still stands. Either way a plurality of independent and separate necessary beings entails mutual limitation and thus mutual dependency even if they were to be isolated from each other.

Ward next argued that their existence could be a contingent necessity at best, because whether interacting (or in isolation) each is in part what it is because of its co-existence with the others. But it could not be even that, because without something else to make at least one of them absolutely necessary the conditions for their existence would not necessarily exist. Nevertheless, this does not itself prove that they are necessary beings, because it may be possible that each could necessarily exist although some of its attributes would be the results of its interaction, or lack of interaction, with the rest. Indeed, Ward later argues that God, the one necessary being, does have contingent attributes arising from his interaction with the world that he has created.[3]

To start again, suppose that there are n necessary beings. But why n? Why not n-1 or n+1, or any other number? There seems to be something arbitrary and merely possible about the whole idea. Each one is supposed to exist necessarily, but where is the necessity for n to exist, and neither any more nor any less? Therefore there must be something distinctive about these n beings such that they and only they exist necessarily, whereas any others would be merely possible. Let us suppose that they have an attribute or a set of attributes, a, such that in virtue of a, they exist necessarily. Hence those beings and only those beings which have a would be necessary ones. But this merely postpones the problem. For then it would be possible that there could be two beings, B_n and B_{mp}, such that they both have attributes b-g but B_n also has a and thus necessarily exists, whereas B_{mp} does not have a and thus exists only merely possibly. But again it seems merely accidental and wholly unnecessary that B_n should have a while B_{mp} does not have a and is merely possible. Nor, of course, could the problem be solved by invoking α in virtue of which B_n has a. Whatever else may or may not be true of necessary being, it cannot be something merely tacked onto the other attributes of a necessary being.

Let us, therefore, suppose that whatever attributes a necessary being has, it has them necessarily. In this way we eliminate the problem of merely possible attributes that make their bearers themselves merely possible. Therefore, if two necessary beings exist, then each will have the same set of necessary attributes as the other. But if that is all that they have, how is the one to be distinguished from the other and what is to make them two and not one? Consequently, each will have to have its own unique and distinguishing attribute, or set of attributes, and to have it or them necessarily. But this is yet again to reinstate the problem that we were trying to solve. For if C can have c to distinguish it from D which has d, then surely there could be E with e, and F with f, and so on, and so it would be a mere possibility that C and D are the only necessary beings. Hence, they would not be necessary after all. It follows that if attributes c-n are necessary involved with necessary existence, then every necessary being must have them all, and, furthermore, no necessary being can have any attributes which any other necessary being does not have nor not have any which any other does have. That is, they must all have exactly one and the same set of necessary attributes. And in that case, there would be nothing to distinguish any one from the others, not even the attribute of not-being-the-others, for without "material" attributes to distinguish them in the first place, this formal attribute would be empty and inapplicable.

The conclusion of all this is inescapable: there cannot be a plurality of necessary beings and so necessary being (a) *is numerically unique,* (b) *has all it properties necessarily,* and (c) *is qualitatively unique in having them all necessarily.* This means that the one necessary being must be totally unlike anything else.

Yet, two objections could be made to this argument. They are that it has made tacit use of the Principle of Sufficient Reason in proposing that there would be no reason for any given one of similar supposedly necessary beings to exist and that we have not suggested, as an answer to that problem, that an infinite number of similar necessary beings could exist, which would eliminate the arbitrariness of the existence of a finite number of them and no less nor any more.

The Principle of Sufficient Reason has long been held as a fundamental axiom and can be stated as that every event that happens or being which exists must have some cause or reason sufficient to bring it about and thus explain its happening or existence. It can be stated as the Principle of Ultimate Intelligibility: that no event or being merely happens or exists as a "brute fact," but always there is something which would fully explain it until we reach that which is self-explanatory, that which cannot not-exist, and whose existence cannot be denied. It can be maintained either as itself a necessary truth into which we have immediate insight or as an absolute presupposition of intellectual enquiry such that it is irrational to stop anywhere short of the ultimate necessity in the process of explanation. It was explicitly formulated by Leibniz who assumed it to mean, as others had done, that a sufficient reason must be such that if A is the sufficient reason for B, then, given A, B must also exist or happen. A sufficient cause or reason, therefore, would be one that wholly determined its effect or result. It follows that everything that exists or happens would exist or happen necessarily. As such, it is understood that the Principle of Sufficient Reason necessarily applies to necessary being. If n necessary beings are held to exist, where $n > 1$, then it does make sense to ask for a reason, why each and all of n identical or similar necessary beings should exist *and no more nor any less*: What exactly is it that makes *these* necessary and not any more? And the reason that is sought must itself be a *necessary* reason, otherwise it would prove only that they can exist and not that they cannot not-exist. But it should be noted in passing that if, as seems obviously the case, merely possible beings can exist, then only some weaker reasons can be given for them, ones that explain why they *can* exist, and perhaps why it is more likely that they should exist than that they should not, but never why they *must* exist.

As for an infinity of necessary beings, that would eliminate the mere possibility of only n actually existing. Note that "infinity," means here the "mathematical infinity" (Hegel's "false infinity") of an unending series. It may be contended that an *actual* infinity is impossible and the idea of it is an illegitimate hypostatisation of the possibility that we can always going on counting or dividing, whereas what exists must be definite in number. Now if is possible for an endless series of entities to exist at the same time, then, it seems, an infinite series of necessary beings would allow for all possible necessary beings to exist and thus would solve the problem of only some and not others. Even so, the members of this unending series would be limited by the others and would have at least some attributes because of the co-existence of the others. If they are all genuinely necessary beings, then, as already demonstrated, all their attributes would have to necessary: they all would have to exist, to have the attributes that they do have, and to be in the mutual relations that they are. If so, the result would not be an infinite series of separate necessary beings, but one necessarily existing, comprehensive, internally, and infinitely differentiated entity. And were they to be wholly separate they would be limited by not being able to interact with each other. Thus, the question would arise as to why they are like this and do not form one infinitely diverse yet wholly integrated being. It would be a merely possible fact that the one arrangement existed and that the other did not.

2. Finitude and Infinity

There can be only one necessary being. It cannot be spatial, because it would have to have one shape and set of colours and not others, and it cannot be temporal because its attributes would be liable to change and thus not necessary. What other sorts of attributes entail finitude and, therefore, cannot be applied to the one necessary being? For the most part they are *exclusive* attributes, ones which exclude others of the same type, such as the spatial and temporal ones already mentioned. To have any of these is to be limited to them and not to have another within the same range. All *quantities*, and everything that is essentially measurable, entail finitude; for to be of one size, length, weight, speed, or duration is not to be of another. So also are all *variable* attributes—whatever they are, they could be otherwise even if they do not vary. Another finite attribute is *situatedness*, existing alongside something else, which need not be confined to being situated in space or time—as with McTaggart's plurality of timeless spirits, or Plato's Demiurge who exists along with the Forms upon which he models the world. For to be in a situation is to be confronted with things which one has not chosen, or not wholly chosen; we never completely create a situation but always find ourselves in it to some extent at least. Hence, they both provide some opportunities, rule out others, and force things upon us, all of which are tokens of our finitude.

Since the one necessary being cannot be finite, then it must be infinite. But that presents serious and long-standing problems. Because the one necessary being cannot have any finite attributes, it is often thought that it cannot have any besides being one and necessary, that is, that it is has a "blank" unity, mere oneness, and is infinite only as being non-finite and is therefore indefinite, mere *being* without being *this* or *that*. The "negative theology" of Pseudo-Dionysius in Europe and that of the more ancient Advaita ("Nondualist") Vendanta school in India expressed it in the same terms: God, the Neo-Platonic One, or Brahma (the Ultimate Being in Hindu thought) is "not this, not that." The assumption underlying all these ways of thinking about the one necessary being was made explicit by Nicholas of Cusa ("Cusanus") and I shall refer to it as "the Cusanian thesis": it is that "*omnis determinatio est negatio*," "all determination is negation." To say what something is, is to "define" it, to "set limits to it," and thus to say what it is not. Hence, the "in-finite" is the "unlimited"; hence "undefined" and "indeterminate"; and hence nothing. Taken literally, the Cusanian thesis would mean that all things are only "not-something-else" and never anything positive in themselves. But usually it has been interpreted as meaning that all "determinations," all descriptive terms, are exclusive, as mentioned above. That is, they do not merely rule out their "privatives"—as "red" rules out "not red"—but all other positive attributes or properties of the same sort, e.g., being red also rules out being green, yellow, blue, etc. The result is that the one necessary being becomes a blank and featureless unity, verging on being indistinguishable from nothingness, as Hegel claimed. Yet Plotinus also affirmed The One to be good and also used personal terms for it; in Advaita Vedantism, Brahman is nevertheless averred to be *sat* (being), *chit* (consciousness), and *ananda* (bliss). Bradley's non-relational Absolute is, all the same, Experience and Spirit; and even the ultimate Void of one school of Buddhism was sometimes said also to be a fullness. Cusanus' way out was to assert that God is the "coincidence of opposites," as if everything that is exclusive could somehow all come together in one non-finite being.

The root problem is the assumption that all attributes, properties, and determinations are exclusive of more than their mere privatives. But consider the possession of knowledge. What does that exclude? Only its privation (ignorance) and its distortion (error). It is they which denote finitude: not knowing when one is able to know, or not being able to know at all, and being mistaken are clearly limitations in themselves and entail further limitations. But knowing itself is wholly positive and non-exclusive. Of course, there have been complaints that knowledge has negative aspects, such as inhibiting action or distorting reality. But the situations and examples adduced are either ones that follow from other limitations (as in the self-consciousness which arises from a fear of making mistakes and disrupts what we intend to do) or are not really forms of knowledge in the first place if they do distort reality. Again, consider moral qualities such as justice and generosity. At first sight, justice may seem to limit generosity by forbidding us to be generous with what we hold in trust for others or have already pledged to other parties. But such generosity is not generosity, for it is not giving freely *of one's own*. What justice inhibits is a specious and immoral generosity such as that of those politicians who take credit for being generous with the taxpayers' money. Far from limiting generosity, justice helps to make it genuine.

But is not knowledge a quantifiable property? For one can know more or less and, therefore, is it not a mark of finitude? Likewise with justice and generosity; these too allow of more and less, and thus must be finite properties of finite persons. If all positive and non-exclusive attributes are quantifiable, then we are once more back where we began: with a blank and empty being that is indistinguishable from nothing.

Here we need to distinguish between "absolute" and "relative" properties or between "absolute" and "relative" attributions of the same property. Some properties, and the terms for them, do not permit of a "more or less" but are or denote a "perfection" or norm *to* which there can be lesser and greater degrees of approximation and *from* which there can be lesser and greater degrees of divergence but *of* which there are no degrees. For example, either a line is straight or it isn't, though empirical lines on close examination will turn out not to be really straight after all. Any line said to be "straighter" than another is, properly speaking, either less crooked or curved than the other or is genuinely straight while the other isn't. These we may call "absolute" properties and terms and as such can qualify, *ceteris paribus*, for attribution to the one necessary being. So too with justice and generosity: our justice and generosity appear to permit of degrees because we are morally and cognitively imperfect. Either in intention or because of limitations upon what we can know, we often do not act truly justly or generously even when we mean to. Materially, our generosity is also limited by our means and other moral commitments, but formally it is limited only by our contrary desires and emotions. Even when we have nothing substantive to give, we can be free of any begrudging desire not to give if we could and of any secret thankfulness that here and now we have left all our money at home. Similarly knowing has a perfect form of completeness and freedom from error, which we do not attain but which the one necessary being could possess. Again, if properties like these can be predicated of the one necessary being, then they would be attributed in their full and perfect and proper forms.

Hence, it can be valid to attribute those positive "determinations" (better "properties" or "attributes") to necessary being which do not entail incompleteness and exclusion of any properties other than their privations or distortions, and which do not entail finitude and mere possibility. As to which such properties we should apply, we have yet to determine.

What we can now say is that the one necessary being cannot be finite, because finitude and mere possibility entail each other. To say that, therefore, it must be "infinite" is not very illuminating (the mere negation of a negation) and may be definitely misleading if we take infinity to be the endless continuation or reduplication of finitude or to be a blank and empty non-being. It would be better to use "transfinite" and "perfect," which imply the transcendence of the limits of finite existence.

3. A Trans-partitive Unity

Positive "determinations," which denote "perfections" or which are attributed in an "absolute" sense, can be predicated of the one necessary being whereas anything else cannot. For that would entail limitation, finitude, and thus mere possibility—being *this* and *not that*. Yet, we coherently cannot think of the one necessary being as having a mere series of attributes, say, *A* to *N*, for it has all its attributes necessarily, as was demonstrated above in §1. It cannot be *A and B and C and D*, etc., in any way that would suggest that it merely happens to have any one and all of them. And this has a definitely positive side, namely, that all the attributes of the one necessary being must follow from its essence, or, rather that they are all its essence for it cannot be other that what it is. Hence, in some way all its attributes must be *one*. But this conclusion appears to return us to the idea of the one necessary being as a blank unity, without differentiation and thus nothing or next to nothing. What is needed is another conception of a unity that is not only more than a mere assemblage but also more than that of a whole of distinguishable parts. For all parts have some relative independence from the whole, in fact as well as in conception: a cog from one mechanism can be used in another; today many organs of one human body can be transplanted into another body; and the lines of the most tightly integrated poem can be partially understood in isolation. On the contrary, we seek a unity that wholly pervades and exists intact in each of its "parts," one which would be the highest degree and form of unity.

Certain facts from our own experience suggest themselves as at least approximations to such a completely non-partitive integration and differentiation. One is the analogy with pure light, which contains and *is* all the many colours that we see refracted or reflected in the things around us. Pure light is not red *and* green *and* blue, etc., yet it is not nothing, which would be utter blackness or the absence of all light. Another set of analogies, comes from personal existence, intentions, and qualities. Firstly, our mental powers (what used to be called "faculties") are not separate and distinct, though at one time one of them may be more prominent than the others: cognition, as when thinking hard about the options in a critical decision; will, as when resolving upon one of them and seeing it through despite setbacks and disappointments; and emotion, as when rejoicing when success is finally achieved. But careful reflection will show that in each of these moments, the others are engaged also, or rather, all mental activity is a unity of functions. For example, knowing requires a desire to know, judgments and decisions about how to find things out, the truth and relevance of evidence, and feelings of satisfaction or dissatisfaction with the results.[4] Even when one function seems to be in conflict with another, as when feeling or emotion is at variance with one's better judgment or "reason," nevertheless emotion has its cognitive structures—its object or objects and the perspective in which they are viewed. There is some feeling attached to the better judgment, otherwise one cannot feel the conflict; it is just that feeling is noticeably stronger on the one side than on the other. Secondly, our intentions necessarily maintain a unity in diversity and change with changing situations precisely in order to remain the same. A commander's intention is to defeat the enemy, but to fulfil it he must at one time attack and at another defend, now advance, and then retreat. And thirdly, it is the same with traits of character which are manifested in many different ways according to different situations: generosity can be a giving of time and attention as well as things; bravery can be better shown in having the moral courage to be called a coward or "chicken" than in doing something reckless in order to avoid such insults. The unity of a course of action or a trait of character is not that of the "material" act but of the "formal" intention. Its differential manifestations are implicit in and are actualised in the appropriate situations as they arise. Hence, Socrates and Plato rightly concluded that virtue is one, though they may have erred in identifying it with the specific virtue of *sophia*. Even more strikingly, the love of parents for their child can and, as the occasion arises, *must* manifest itself in ways that may seem to the child to be quite opposed to it—as when they do not give him what he asks for or chastise him for what he has done wrong. Their love, in order to be genuine love and not indulgence nor a craving to be loved, is directed to the child's good and hence can issue in "material" actions seemingly akin to those of coldness or anger and not love at all. Such conceptions and analogies we shall need to raise to a higher power in transferring them to the one necessary being *all* of whose attributes must be implicit and contained in each other. From our point of view, they may appear as manifold and thus to be integrated, but from that of the one necessary being, they are one and itself.

4. Eternity

The one necessary being cannot be temporal, for it has all its attributes necessarily, and so it cannot cease to exist, cease to be what it is, or become more or less. This was Parmenides' insight: the one reality is "(It) Is!" Likewise God revealed himself to Moses as, "I am Who am," and Aquinas named him as "He Who Is" and as Pure Act without any unrealised potentialities. In Hindu metaphysics Brahman is *sat*, "is-ness" or being. Only from *our point of view*, that is within time, do we say that the one necessary being always *was* and always *will be* (as in the alternative rendition of "I am who am" as "I will be what I will be"). From its or his point of view, it or he simply *is*.

Hence we must clearly distinguish between mere everlastingness (or immortality in the case of personal beings) and eternity proper. "Everlastingness" signifies merely that the existence of the being in question will not end. Such an unending existence may be thoroughly temporal and not eternal. Temporality has three dimensions: past, present, and future; what was, what is, and what will be. To be temporal is thus to have been something, to be something else, and to be about to be something different again. On the one side of what one (for the moment) is, there was a *no longer*, and on the other there will be a *not yet*. It is change, and thus loss and gain, that constitutes temporality: becoming, and so becoming less or more or both, in different respects. Such a process of change, becoming no longer and not yet, and gain and loss, could continue without end, as in those beliefs in a life after death which envisage it as essentially a continuation of this, albeit a better one, but not radically different, and as in Kant's of an endless striving for a moral perfection which we can approach but never attain. In contrast, eternity (in the proper sense) is a state above and beyond change, becoming, and temporality, without any no longer or not yet. It is a state of *being* without *having been* or *being about to be*.

But to our minds, activity tends to suggest change, doing one thing, then another, and so on. Each action has a beginning and an end. Especially if we assume, as empiricist and utilitarian philosophers do, that all action is a means to attain an end-state beyond itself, then it is a necessary truth that all activity is self-terminating. But this is to ignore Aristotle's important distinction between *genesis* and *energeia*,[5] between, respectively, a *process* of change towards a goal beyond the process, at the attainment of which the process ends—as house building terminates when the house is built, and the continuing *activity* of a complete and unimpaired function or power, such as the regular beating of a healthy heart or the faultless playing of an expert musician. In the performance of an activity, there is of course change, and change at several levels—such as the alternation of systole and diastole in the heart, the sequence of notes in the piece played, the greater or lesser pace of beating when an animal is active or at rest, and the change of tempo and style within the piece of music and from one piece to another. But these changes on a higher level are the proper responses to changes in the circumstances of the heart or the musician. It would be an impaired heart or unskillful musician who could not adapt to them, and therefore would need to change to be able to do so. A change such as this would be what Plato called a *genesis eis ousian*, a "becoming (or process) into being,"[6] that is, a change which is more and more incremental, more and more gain and less and less loss until the performance is perfect—which at the highest level does not change at all because it is all that it could be. Its self-adaptation on lower levels to changes in circumstances would be spontaneous, effortless, and flawless, as by a pianist who could immediately and faultlessly play any score set before him, including those by Liszt which even he, as he admitted, could play only on his better days. Now, such a final state may be achievable by bodily organs though, of course, they are always vulnerable and will sooner or later decay and die along with the whole organism, but for finite persons there is always more to be added. New pieces can be added to one's repertoire and there is new music yet to be composed, and new techniques to be acquired. For the one necessary being, there would never be anything more to be added. Let alone any possibility of loss or need for improvement, because it would always be everything it could be. Therefore, its existence would be one seamless and unchanging activity. This, we can experience in part and imagine only in terms of a continuing rhythm, an unchanging pattern of regular changes in detail. It is rhythm, not time *per se*, that is "the moving image of eternity."[7] To our imaginations a wholly static, inert, and "frozen" existence appears exactly the same as one of wholly unchanging activity, but it may be the case that we can legitimately conceive of objects which we cannot imagine. Even if that is not so, it would remain that the one necessary being performs or *is* a complete, and hence unchanging, pattern of activity of rhythmical changes in its detail.

5. Analogy and Metaphor

In the next chapter, we shall consider further and more specifically personal attributes of the one necessary being. But first a question that has often arisen and will continue to do so: How we can speak intelligibly of the one necessary being that transcends all our thought and language, especially in view of the apophatic "not this, not that" of the *via negativa*? Since I have elsewhere said all that I have to say, following Michael Polanyi, about the general problems of speaking about that which transcends all our thought and action,[8] I shall now merely restate three principal points about language. These points show that even in respect of familiar, finite existence our language is always and necessarily inexact, less than what we can know, and created, controlled, and extended by our essentially tacit understanding of what we mean by it.

All language is inadequate and must be so otherwise it could not function. A truly *precise* use of language would exactly fit the reality it referred to. But then, as Polanyi said, it would be like the map that exactly copies the landscape at the scale of 1:1 and so would be useless as a map. "Precision engineering" is only less imprecise than ordinary engineering—for, if there were no tolerances or slacks at all, nothing would move. So too with language: all of it is imprecise and some modes are only less imprecise than others or only in certain respects. For example, mathematics is precise and unequivocal, but, as every working scientist knows, the neat equations and curves of scientific theory are an abstraction from and an idealsation of the experimental results that approximate to them. Better instrumentation may refine measurements and reduce discrepancies, but they can never eliminate it. And in human reality, while mathematical economists may make all manner of precise deductions from their curves, all applied economics is informed guesswork as to what is happening and is likely to happen. The very precision of mathematics in economic theory can be dangerously illusory in practice. Since nothing is wholly "effable," the ineffability of the one necessary being is not quite the problem that it may have been thought to be.

Pace, the earlier Wittgenstein, nothing can be said with complete clarity; and *pace,* the later Wittgenstein, thought is not confined to language. If it were, then the bounds of our language would be those of our world and we could neither think nor know of that of which we could not speak: no word for it, no idea of it, and no knowledge of it. How then could language arise in the first place and grow in the second, and be corrected in the third? I can search for and find *le mot juste* and discard inadequate words only because I tacitly know what I am trying to say. Hence, I can discover and think of things for which there are as yet no words and, as with the one necessary being, that for which all our words are inadequate. The *via negativa* of saying "not this, not that," presupposes this prior power of tacit apprehension, which generates and controls all our language—for one can responsibly say what something *is not* only with some knowledge of what it *is*.

Theologians in the Thomist tradition have rightly supplemented the *via negativa* with the doctrine of analogy, so that terms to be applied to God are to be understood "eminently," that is, as signifying a perfect form of what they attribute and not the imperfect forms which apply to finite entities. Yet, it seems to me, they sometimes wrongly concede the priority and normatively of "literal" meaning and still regard analogy and metaphor as somehow anomalous. On the contrary, it is allegedly literal meaning that is the anomaly. For it is in fact metaphor so dead that it is erroneously thought never to have been alive. Consult an etymological dictionary for any word and you will find that today's "literal" meaning began as an analogical or metaphorical extension of a previous meaning that has now replaced an earlier meaning as the standard (witness "prevent," which in the seventeenth century still meant "go before," and Milton's puns on contemporary and previous meanings). Once every word was a new coinage and had no "literal" meaning—as it still is for one encountering it for the first time. As with today's analogies, metaphors, and new coinages, the speaker has to rely on the ability of his audience tacitly to grasp what he is trying to say by means of it—to attend *from* the word itself and *to* that to which it is being used to refer. The transcendence of our thought and language by the one necessary being is of another order altogether, yet, is not wholly dissimilar.

Notes

1. See *The Nature of Existence*, Vol. II, esp. Chs. XXXIX and XL, or the summary in his contribution to *Contemporary British Philosophy*, 2nd Series. McTaggart does not explicitly state that the society of spirits exists necessarily, but, having shown to his satisfaction that time is unreal, he rightly concludes that spirits are timeless. He also argues that all selves are primary parts of the universe and thus "fundamental," "ultimate facts"; that the universe is not a self; and that no self can contain or create any others. Hence, his is an ultimate pluralism.

2.   See also below, Ch. 4 §5.
3.   See also below, Ch. 6 §3.
4.   See my "Governance by emotion" (*J. of the Brit. Soc. for Phenomenology*, Vol. 22 No. 2, May 1991, 15-30) for the role of emotion in all action and "The cognitive functions of emotion," (*Appraisal*, Vol. 3 No. 1, March 2000, 38-47; *Polanyiana*, Vol. 15, No.s 1-2, 2006, 21-40) on its roles in knowing. See also St. Augustine's study of the mutual involvement of memory, understanding, and will in *De Trinitate*, Bk X.
5.   *Nichomachean Ethics*, 1157b, 35.
6.   *Philebus*, 26d.
7.   *Timaeus*, 37c.
8.   *Transcendence and Immanence*, Ch. 5.

4

Impersonal or Personal?

1. Ideal Existence

In the previous chapter it was shown that certain other attributes—being one and not many, having all attributes necessarily, perfection and not finitude, a non-partitive but self-differentiating unity, eternity—follow from necessary existence. At first sight, it seems that it cannot be so clearly demonstrated that further properties, such as being personal, also follow from necessary existence. Yes, anything that implies finitude can be ruled out, but there appears to be no positive criterion for deciding what could also apply to the one necessary being. But, since it has been shown to possess all its attributes necessarily, what *can* apply to it *must apply* to it. Therefore, all that we need to ask about any additional candidates for its attributes is whether they entail finitude or not: if they do, they cannot apply; and if they do not, they must apply.

Traditionally, the options for fundamental forms of existence have been matter and mind or spirit. Physical existence can be ruled out for it entails spatiality, which entails finitude. But we cannot therefore infer that the one necessary being must be a mind or spirit. For a third mode of being has sometimes been proposed, that of ideal existence such as a Platonic Idea or Form.[1] We, therefore, need to examine if such a conception is coherent and, if it is, if it entails finitude.

It has sometimes been argued that the objects of logical, mathematical, and moral judgments must be about a realm of ideal or logical entities, neither physical nor mental. How else could they be true or false, valid or invalid, except by corresponding to such things, just as perceptual judgments are true or false as corresponding to the things perceived? But does this analogy hold? Consider our knowledge of the past, and especially the pre-human past, when there was no one around to perceive it at the time. Our knowledge of such things is inferred *from* what can

31

be perceived now—documents, surviving artefacts, fossils, rock strata, etc.—but is mostly not *of* things that can be perceived now. Our knowledge of the number series and moral and logical norms is of objects that cannot be perceived at all but only conceived. Must it therefore be of a special realm of imperceivable objects, ghostly simulacra of perceptible ones? I see no reason to suppose so. For what sorts of *entity* could a valid formula or inference, or a moral value or law be? Indeed, what sort of thing is the law of the land? It is not what is written in a statute book, for there were laws long before there was writing, and they would remain the laws even if the official record of them were destroyed. Their reality is that of objects conceived and agreed to be the laws binding upon the respective group of persons. As for moral and other norms, a form of justice conceived on the model of a perceptible object would be a mere thing and not a norm and something which we should obey. It itself would be not just, for only persons can be just. Rather, the archetypes of moral, logical, and other norms would be the conduct and thinking of an absolutely moral and rational person, as was acknowledged by Christian Platonism, which interpreted the previously impersonal Platonic Forms as Ideas in the mind of God. In any case, a realm of merely ideal or logical objects would be a finite one because it would be impotent; values, laws, and norms cannot *do* anything. This, Plato tacitly recognised when, as well as the system of Forms, he also conceived of the Demiurge who would be able to model a world upon them. Hence, even if a realm of forms, or logical and ideal objects could exist, it could not be the one necessary being, nor could the latter exist in that mode.

2. Mental or Spiritual Existence

In the absence of another conceivable mode of existence, only mental or spiritual existence remains. If that can be attributed to the one necessary being, then it must be attributed, as argued above. These days, because of widespread resistance to any "dualism," we cannot immediately ask if the one necessary being is a purely mental or spiritual being, but first we must endeavour to make an independent case for a pluralism of essence or types of being, and to show that the idea of a purely spiritual being is self-consistent in the first place. This is not the place for a full treatment of these questions, and we must content ourselves with the essential points at issue.

1. The Distinctiveness of Mental Existence

An insistence that all existence not only is but *must* be physical, hardly squares with a positivist rejection of all metaphysics or with that of empiricism, which rejects all necessary connections in reality. What we have here appears to be a fundamental but unargued assumption against which we can set a more genuine empiricism that is sensitive to all our experience and which will not foreclose the issue at the outset.

Many of the essential characteristics of mental or spiritual existence bear no reference to space and physical existence: thoughts, memories, imaginations, expectations, decisions, intentions, attitudes, emotions, and desires cannot have shape, weight, colour, or position, though their objects may have them. Furthermore, what is distinctive of mind is meaning; and, though physical entities and events can have meanings, meaning is not any or any set of physical properties nor the function of them. Any pattern of sound, shape, colour, movement, smell, or taste can have a meaning or lack meaning altogether and bear a particular meaning such as "danger" or "mother." Meaning, though carried for us by physical entities and events, is itself beyond the physical through which we express it and in which we read it.

Mental acts cannot be correlated with distinct patterns of behaviour (e.g., fear can result in such diverse "behaviours" as flight, freezing and "playing dead," paralysis, counter-attack, and pre-emptive strike) and have yet to be correlated with distinct states or processes in the brain. Even if we could *correlate* them, that would prove that we recognise each side independently of the other and, thus, that we could not *identify* them with each other: in a monogamous society there is an exact correlation of currently married men with currently married women but that does not show that husbands are the same as wives. On the contrary, correlation presupposes non-identity.

It is sometimes objected, as by Passmore,[2] that any pluralism of essence, of distinct orders of being, is untenable because any supposed relation between them can be explained only terms of one of them if there is an ontological gap between them. Each world, or order, or level of being has its own laws and powers that are confined to it and so cannot apply to any other. Hence, if we do distinguish mind and matter, we must explain any interaction in either mental or physical terms, for there would be nothing in the one relevant to the mode of action of the other: the body is subject only to physical processes and the mind can employ only rational means such as persuasion. In the present case, the choice would be between idealism (better, mentalism) and materialism. The result would be in each case a reductionism,which as Passmore explicitly declares, eliminates any possibility of different levels or orders of reality. But the very same argument would apply equally to any pluralism of the same species: even if *A* and *B* are of the same order of being, any explanation of the action of the one upon the other would have to be in terms of one of them alone for there could be nothing in either to allow of the other's action upon it. If (rightly) it is proposed that it is part of *A*'s nature to be susceptible to being affected by others like it, such as *B*, and likewise of *B*, so that any action is simultaneously an action of the one and a reaction of the other, then equally it can be the case that it is in the nature of one order of existence to be able to act upon another order and to be susceptible to being acted upon by it, so that, again, any interaction is an explanation in terms of both. It simply begs the questions to assert that mind, when embodied, cannot also use and be affected by physical powers; and that a body, when "minded," cannot affect and be affected by mental powers. That is what we experience, and, contrary to what Passmore states, the interaction that we experience is across an ontological gap, as shown above. If anyone's ontological framework declares this to be impossible, than, as with the physics that entails that bumblebees cannot fly, it is the framework or theory that is wrong. As for how such interaction operates, I would point to Polanyi's account of the tacit integration of levels by dual control in which the operational principles of each higher level determine the boundary conditions left open by the previous lower level.[3]

Hence, we must recognise mind as a mode of being distinct from, though capable of, accompanying and interacting with physical existence.

2. The Real Errors of "Dualism"

So far we have been operating with a dualism of mind (or spirit) and body. Now whatever else may be said about Descartes' philosophy, his was definitely such an ontology. Whether all the other elements of "dualism" were also his, I shall not determine.

What is primarily wrong with "dualism" is not that it distinguishes two orders of existence instead of one, but that it distinguishes *only* two. For between body and mind is the great missing third of organic *life*: remember that for Descartes animals were but automata and he gave no consideration to his own living and lived body, that which is alive or dead, healthy or ill, whole or impaired, immature or mature or senescent, fertile or infertile. These, and the processes of nutrition, digestion, and excretion, of growth and decay, of reproduction, of self-differentiation into diverse but mutually supporting functions and organs and organic systems are the essential and distinctive features of life that set it above merely physical existence and introduce into it the distinction of organism and environment. And above mind is the even more important and missing fourth (though Descartes' with his *cogito, sum*, should have recognised it) that of the *person*, the one who *uses* his mind, who can be "out of it" when it functions automatically without his responsible and responsive direction, and in partial abeyance when he is deeply asleep or when it is used by another as in hypnotism. Within these orders of existence we may need to distinguish suborders. The important point is that we need to be open to the diversity of reality and our experience of it and not to distort it with an *a priori* and reductive ontology.

The other error in what is called "dualism" is that of equating interaction with causation. It has been widely and for a long time supposed that there are two parallel series of events—the one mental and the other bodily. Earlier events in each series cause both later ones in the same series and, at times, also in the other series. Thus, events in the nervous system were supposed to cause sensations in the mind, which in turn cause feelings of attraction or aversion, which in turn cause movements towards or away from that which caused the events in the nervous system in the first place. The mental series is taken to be observable only by the individual in his own case, and his knowledge of others' minds is thus held to be an inference from their observable behaviour to its hidden causes on the analogy of the observed links between his own mental and bodily events. Now, because the two events are assumed to be quite different in nature, these inferences have rightly become suspect and so solipsism has proved to be the logical result of this model. Hence, to avoid that, it has been maintained that mental events either are identified with observable bodily ones or are taken to be an unknowable and not really relevant linkage among observable bodily events (you do not need to know how your television works in order to turn it on and select a channel). The choice, then, is between solipsism and "nulipsism"—either every event is wholly private to one self, *my* self, or there are no selves but only publicly observable behaviour. (Naturally, the question of how behaviour can be observed when there are no observers is never raised.) But in reality the primary relation between mind and body, or rather between both and personal or sub-personal centre, is that of *expression*.

My body is primarily not an *object* of my action but its instrument and vehicle. It is that with and through which I act upon the world and express myself to myself and to others. My intentions *embody* themselves in actions, which I monitor, control, and adapt, and are not interior, antecedent "causes" or the mere movements themselves. Tiredness *lives* in the droop, pride in the upright stance, happiness and tenderness in the smile. Stance, gesture, facial appearance, and tone of voice are the primary language—that of emotion, desire, intention, calling, and commanding—which we all recognise and respond to. They are the direct expressions of the person, its essential ingredients and vehicles, and not mere causal, casual, and distinct *effects*. I mention this, not because it is directly relevant, but because the obsession with causation blinds us to the real relation between person and body and, thus, reinforces prejudices against any distinction between them.

3. Purely Mental or Spiritual Existence

Acknowledging the reality of different orders of existence is one thing, and envisioning them as existing apart may be another. Nevertheless, those who insist that mind cannot exist without matter argue beyond experience, for constant conjunction in our experience does not by itself prove logical and ontological inseparability. In support of the necessary dependence of mind upon matter, it is sometimes argued that without bodies we could not identify minds. But that is exactly what we can do. Consider the attribution of authorship to a text: we do not have Shakespeare physically with us, but it is still possible to determine that *Henry VIII* is but partly his work and partly that of another, probably Fletcher. Likewise, no references at all were made to any bodies when Biblical scholars distinguished First from Second Isaiah, and then those from the probably several prophets who contributed to Third Isaiah, nor when it was definitely recognised that not St. Paul but someone else was the author of *Hebrews*. As the French say, the style is the man, and literary style is not a physical phenomenon.

We may go further. Let us imagine that our experience were to consist wholly of sounds, as it almost does when one listens intently to the wireless. Now, although sounds in our real world are carried and received by physical means, for our experiment we can think that away and imagine being in a world that consists solely of sound and the persons who send and receive them. As one distinguishes one real or fictitious person on the wireless from another by tone of voice and the contents and style of what is said, so too in our imaginary world we would be able to distinguish different voices and hence persons. This is, in fact, our experience of people we encounter only as voices on the radio or telephone and, for the blind, of all those whom they do not touch.[4] After all, the identity of a text has no physical basis. It can exist in any number and kind of physical entities and, for all those centuries before writing was invented, it was embodied solely in human memory and speech. Its identity is an identity of *meaning*, and meaning is not a physical entity, property, or relation.

Hence, mental or spiritual existence is not essentially tied to bodily existence; therefore, in that respect there is nothing to stop us from attributing it to the one necessary being. But perhaps there are other respects in which it is incompatible with necessary being.

3. Impersonal Consciousness

Yes, the one necessary being *can* be mind and consciousness and therefore *must* be such. But is it therefore personal? Can there be such a being as an impersonal mind or conscious? There are at least four ways in such a conception has been formed, or alleged to have been formed, and we shall now briefly review them to see if they prove coherent.

As in Popper's "Third World," knowledge is often supposed to be something that can be stored in such physical objects as books, photographs, computer disks, etc. This is not even impersonal mind but mindless knowledge. It will suffice to point out the obvious, that any such knowledge is merely potentially knowledge which becomes actual only when read, seen, or heard by someone who *understands* it and *believes* it. Nothing written or recorded in Chinese can by itself impart knowledge to me, and Popper himself would not have accredited as knowledge a book of astrology.

What Polanyi called "Objectivism" would make knowledge almost wholly a function of the object known and of a comprehensive set of self-applying rules such as a complete casuistry or computer program. Here we would have simply consciousness, bare awareness, and none of the other personal attributes or activities such as judgment, interpretation, and appraisal. To some extent, the otherwise devastating criticisms made of such a conception are beside the point in the present context, because they focus upon our passionate engagement, as finite persons, in a world which we need to *discover* and do not make.[5] Nevertheless the essential objections still apply. For while the one necessary being is the full integration of what we experience in dispersed and partial forms, personal involvement is necessary in all modes of knowing. It is not the case, for example, that we need to have a firm commitment to intellectual integrity simply to thwart our propensities to self-deception, sloppy and fallacious inference, rash and arbitrary assumptions, and the like. For apart from such defects and temptations, any knowledge would not be *our own* if we did not, tacitly at least, accredit and uphold it. It would be, as far as we were concerned, something external and unimportant. You could operate a logical system wholly in accordance with its rules, and those rules could be correct rules for inference, but without personal *validation* of those rules, your operation of them would be only a game—just like a child's random cranking of a mechanical calculator or a parrot's recitation of the two-times table. The Objectivist model is, ultimately, one of personal passivity. Ideally our minds would be automata, mechanically processing data just like computers. In such a case, they would not be *our* minds for *we* would be not involved in them in any way. The question is, Could there be any mind which did not, explicitly or tacitly, validate its knowledge as knowledge? Consider the *epoché*, the suspension of judgment, of ancient scepticism. Even if I could suspend judgment about the perceived world, I could not suspend judgment about suspending judgment because I would still be judging and validating as successful or not my suspensions of judgment about what I perceive. Aristotle's God, absorbing in thinking about thinking, must necessarily endorse the validity of what genuine thinking is, both as the object of his knowledge and as his own exercise of it.

A third possibility is the older tradition of Rationalist monism, which often explicitly draws a significant consequence implied by Objectivism as well. If, as assumed by both, knowing is taken to be a process of logical deduction or calculation or dialectical expansion, it then follows that, given the same premises (the same inputs) to the system and the correct operation of that system, the same processes will be followed and same conclusions reached by all minds. With the additional assumption that the mind is individualised only by its contents, it then follows that all minds would really be *one* mind. It can therefore be only our inevitably differing locations in space and time (even Siamese twins do not share exactly the same physical location and orientation) which differentiates the one mind into many minds, many modes of its one substance. Time and again Max Scheler complained of this set of assumptions as in Avicenna, Averoës, Spinoza, Kant (at least implicitly), Fichte, and Hegel.[6] Clear statements of this monism were also made by Bernard Bosanquet.[7]

For the present purpose, it is not the monism of this metaphysics that matters,[8] but its impersonalism. The one mind is only the system of logical implication or dialectical development, not so much eternally rehearsed as eternally self-rehearsing. For, whether the system of implication or development were an object distinct from the one mind (and we have seen, in §1 above, such a conception is highly problematical) or a system of thoughts within and thought by that mind, it could not move anything else and so it could not be *merely* contemplated but would have to be actively thought and thought out, and therefore willed and validated by the one mind. Either way, the one mind would not be only awareness but also personally active.

Finally, "Strong Artificial Intelligence," the contemporary equivalent of impersonal monism, asserts that minds are like computers and operate according to sets of algorithms. It follows, though this corollary is not drawn, that, given the same set of algorithms and the same inputs, the same outputs will result, barring damage to the physical mechanisms in which they are embedded. Strong AI results from a "linguistic inversion": mental terms such as "know," "information," and "decide," are applied as "reduced" metaphors and analogies to the operations of computers. The reduction of those meanings, as thus applied, is then forgotten or ignored; and, because mental terms are now taken be literally applicable to computers, computers are said literally to be able to think and to be conscious—and minds are held to be and to operate in the same way as computers, that is, by sets of algorithms. Its other specific error is its omission of the necessity for *personal* judgment and decision, on the part of designers, programmers, and users, about the suitability of computer programs for their tasks, the validity of their logic, the accuracy of their inputs, and the interpretation and the validity of their outputs. For programs can be badly designed and unfit for how they are to be used. They can have faulty logic in the sense of the specific logic of its application (mathematics, accountancy, production or stock control, etc.) and also poor use of logic in the computer language used. They could become corrupted with use and malfunction because of faults in the hardware. That something has been produced by a computer does not guarantee its infallibility.[9] No matter how far these tasks may themselves be computerised, both that process of computerisation and also the continuing operation of the programs produced require personal judgment and decision in the very same ways.

In none of these systems is there a *person* who thinks, judges, and decides. But they all have to allow that a mind, or a computer, can be conscious of itself; otherwise, these accounts of it could not be formulated. And self-consciousness presupposes a consciousness that can pay attention to *itself* and so there is a *self*, a unity, and not just a concatenation of forces or a series of transient states or set of algorithms. If the one necessary being were to be conscious but not conscious of itself, then it would indeed be finite, and so also would it be if it were like us and not *fully* self-conscious and wholly transparent to itself. And what is finite cannot belong to necessary being.

4. Choice and Responsibility

Self-consciousness and choice and responsibility imply each other. We cannot be responsible for our actions if we cannot be aware of them either directly or indirectly, as by noting their effects; if we are aware of them, we are responsible for them—once I become aware of something about myself, I can at least choose to try to alter it, and so freedom and choice are also involved. But can freedom and choice apply to the one necessary being? Choice presupposes a set of items *from* which we can choose and, therefore, a situation in which there are two or more courses of action open to the chooser. The essential problem is that choices are made among *possibilities*. I am faced with choices because I cannot do everything at once even among my purely mental acts. I can never simultaneously be all that I can be, quite apart from external constraints, for mine is an essentially serial and finite existence. But that does not apply to the one necessary being, who is necessarily, simultaneously, and eternally what he is and is without any unrealised possibilities. There is nothing for him to choose between, not because of the paucity of the menu but because of his utter fullness. He is above choice, and is not subject to any limitations or external necessities. In that respect, he cannot do otherwise, but not in any limiting sense as if it were imposed upon him. We experience a transcendence of the opposition of freedom and necessity when we freely do what we love to do, or in which a course of action presents itself as a necessity, as when ungrudgingly accepting an overriding duty. In contrast, the victims of addiction and fascination, on some occasions at least, feel driven against their will and experience self-loathing because of this.[10]

Choice and responsibility imply or presuppose each other. I am responsible for my choices, and if I cannot choose, I cannot be responsible. Responsibility for oneself and one's actions also requires responsibility to something beyond oneself, namely, a law, set of standards, value, or ideal in the light of which one judges one's own conduct. Here we meet the paradox of choice: it requires not only possibilities *from* which to choose, possibilities which have not been chosen, but also a set of preferences *by* which we choose and which we have not chosen. No matter what is on the menu, I can choose from it only insofar as I prefer one dish to another or any dish to eating nothing at all. Consequently, to choose a set of preferences, standards, values, ideals, etc., would presuppose a prior set of preferences, standards, values, ideals, etc. It therefore seems as if we are stuck with the old problem of Plato's *Euthyphro*: either something is good simply because God or the one necessary being wills it (theological positivism) or God wills it because it is good independently of his will. Now the problem with theological positivism and with its successor, legal positivism, is that it must appeal, at least tacitly, to a natural law or basic norm—*not* of God's or the state's making, according to which we should obey whatever God wills or whatever the state legislates and the courts decide. And the problem with the latter alternative is that God must stand under the Form of the Good, the Natural Law or the objective order of values just as we finite persons do and, hence, himself be finite. Or we could deny the problem by insisting that the one necessary being is "beyond good and evil," responsibility and irresponsibility and, hence, beyond personhood. But, if so, "beyond" would really mean "below."

Christian Platonism avoided this dilemma by bringing the Ideas or the fundamental norms of conduct within the one necessary being or God. Yet this looks like an *ad hoc* and artificial expedient, an attempt to combine two very different orders of being, the spiritual being of the one necessary being or God with the purely "logical" existence of the Forms, Natural Law, the objective order of values or the fundamental norms. It also suggests that the latter is still something *given* to the one necessary being or God and, thus, introducing an element of finitude. So is there some way in which we can genuinely combine these two seemingly irreconcilable demands: that the one necessary being does not arbitrarily will or legislate what is good, right, etc., and yet that they are not independent of the one necessary being and the one necessary being thus subject to them?

As was argued in §1 above, laws and norms cannot be hypostasized into existences in their own right and only a person could be the exemplar of logic, mathematical, and other thinking and of moral qualities. For only a person can be logical, correct in thinking and virtuous, and also can manifest all the tacit details, modifications, exceptions, and so on, that elude any explicit codification—hence, the importance of admired models, saints, and heroes alive, dead, legendary, or fictional.

Consequently, the one necessary being, necessarily existing and being what it is, *is* the pattern of and for personal life—the full exemplar of all the virtues and that in their unity.[11] There can be no question that the one necessary being is not good, just, merciful, etc.

Yet, it may once more seem that the necessity of the one necessary being's attributes makes them less than personal. The one necessary being cannot but be righteous, just, etc., and so has no choice in the matter. As shown above, this necessity is neither external nor imposed. St. Augustine distinguished, on the one hand, between the *posse non peccare* (or power not to sin) which we now possess along with the *posse peccare* (or power to sin) and, on the other, the *posse non peccare* which is not a sub-personal incapacity for both good and evil but such a total adhesion to good in heart and mind, that any idea of failing to be good or doing evil is utterly abhorrent. That is the moral ideal that we fallen creatures have yet to achieve but which God or the one necessary being eternally enjoys. It is a failure to rise above meta-*physics* to the meta-personal that lies behind the inability to distinguish the "physical" necessity that is imposed and about which we can do nothing from the "moral" necessity in which necessity is itself a free and personal act, as in Luther's *"Ich kann nicht anders."*

5. Goodness and Finitude

But in all of the above we have been assuming that goodness, and specifically moral goodness, is properly attributable to the one necessary being. There have been several accounts of goodness or value which would render that impossible, and so we need briefly to review them.

One common idea of the good is that which satisfies desire. And one very common understanding of desire is that it is *wanting* and thus is self-contradictory, for as soon as one obtains what one wants, one no longer wants it. Hence, the idea of good as that which would satisfy desire is also self-contradictory and cannot be realised, let alone within necessary being.[12] The initial premise is itself an error, for it makes it impossible to desire anything because it is good and not worthless or bad. But, setting that aside, this contention trades on a fatal ambiguity in "want." For "want" means both "desire" and "lack," and thus from wanting as desiring we can pass all too easily to wanting as lacking, and thus to the assumption that to desire is always to lack, with the result that desire is always suicidal and unsatisfiable. That conclusion also trades on the common experience of disappointment, which seems to give it empirical support, especially when fleeting objects are desired as in Hobbes' "restless desire for power after power." Yet again, it trades on the fact, or apparent fact, that "want" is used when one does not have what one desires. For there is less need to say that we desire what we already have, than to say that we desire what we presently lack. But another who lacks and desires what I now have, will ask me, "Do you want X?" My answer, whether, "yes" or "no," does not refer to my *lack* of X, but to my *desire* for X; for if he thought I lacked X, he would not have asked me if I wanted it. Desire satisfied is precisely that, and desire terminated is something else—for one thing, it can be terminated without being satisfied, as by withering and dying. Satisfaction and contentment are precisely the having, not the losing, of what one desires. The one necessary being, never lacking anything, is eternally satisfied.

A second misconception is that opposing concepts must be both applicable or neither can be: so that for there to be light, there must also be dark; for there to be truth, there must also be error; for there to be good, there must also be bad or evil.[13] A particular application of this misconception is the negative conception of moral good which makes it essentially and only the removal of evil, and hence suicidal: we could term it "the reformist fallacy." According to it, one can be good only in fighting against evil within or without oneself.[14] So that, just at the point when one has overcome the last elements of evil, one ceases to be good or to have any good to do, just like Dorothea in the opening chapters of *Middlemarch*. The good will, in this theory, is essentially self-frustrating and must be secretly glad that evil still exists. Good is hence parasitic upon evil and so finite. But this is like saying that teaching consists only in correcting errors: so that once pupils no longer make mistakes there is nothing more to be taught, or that once one has mastered a craft or skill one therefore can no longer practise it. On the contrary, the bad and the evil are destructive of the good and not mere lack of it (the error of the "privative" theory of evil) which is worthlessness, a zero value. Evil is that which counteracts the good and prevents, stunts, thwarts, impairs, and destroys it. Hence, it must both have something good to attack and itself employ what is generally good, such as strength and, on the personal level, insight, intelligence, commitment, and discipline. Had the KGB and its predecessors, the Gestapo and the SS, and even more so the parties that created and employed them, been bunches of bumbling clowns or each out only for himself, the world would have been spared a great deal of suffering. It is disease that preys upon health, and not health which requires disease. Error requires knowledge—the illiterate cannot misspell anything—and knowledge does not feed on error. Good, therefore, is positive; worthlessness is lack of good; and evil is that which works against good. Good is, therefore, a positive and non-exclusive attribute and so, in all its forms, moral and non-moral can *ceteris paribus* and therefore *must* be predicated of the one necessary being.

Yet, we may be reminded, there are virtues which presuppose the existence of evil: one cannot be compassionate to those who do not suffer, nor merciful to those who are not sinners. And there are other virtues which cannot be predicated of the one necessary being: for example, courage, fortitude, and endurance, which can be displayed only by one who is *vulnerable*, who can be less than what he now is, and perhaps cease to exist. Consequently, to display or enact all the virtues, the one necessary being *needs* other persons and also the evil among and within some of them. Therefore, with them he would be brought down to finitude and so to the modality of merely possible being, or without them would remain incomplete and, hence, finite and so again merely possible. Whichever way we turn, the one necessary being must be finite after all. The answer to this dilemma is the unity of virtue, as mentioned in Ch. 3 §3 as an analogy for the completely integrated unity of the one necessary being. But now that we have demonstrated that the one necessary being is personal, the unity of virtue, of mental functions and of intention are no longer analogies. The specific virtues can be only specifications of the one virtue, the way it is manifested in specific circumstances or towards specific objects. Complete and unswerving devotion to good and right manifests itself as courage in situations of danger, as fortitude and endurance in those of hardship, as compassion in relation to the sufferings of others, as justice in relation to their rights, and so on. And taken and regarded as distinct, these specific forms fall away from virtue and cease to be virtuous: courage has no value in pursuit of an evil cause; justice by itself becomes merely backward looking to what has been done for good or ill;[15] compassion without justice can rob Peter to relieve Paul; mercy without justice becomes indulgence. Therefore, while not to display the appropriate specific virtue in a relevant situation is a severe moral fault, it does not follow that one who never encounters such a situation lacks that specific form. If we all were to behave properly towards each other, *acts* of forbearance and forgiveness would not be required, but the *dispositions* to forbear and forgive the wrongdoings of others would still be implicit in our fundamental orientation to the good. It is that central and unifying intention or fundamental disposition that matters. Hence virtues, such as courage and fortitude, which can be displayed only by finite persons are implicit in the total exemplification of good that is the one necessary being.

5. Not Simply One but Also Two

Nevertheless, the unity of virtue is not a complete answer to the problems just raised. For, apart from the errors of separating out distinct virtues and of the need for others in distress or committing evil, it still remains that certain central intentions require the existence of others, for example, generosity; one cannot give except to others. Above all one central attribute of personhood which cannot be intra-personal, not even for the one necessary being, is that complete devotion to good of which we have already spoken. For all devotion is giving and complete devotion is giving oneself; one cannot give anything *to* oneself. Moreover, one cannot fully give oneself except to another person. There is no reciprocity at all in a mere ideal, Form or Law, and though a dog may give itself wholly to its master, the master cannot give himself wholly to his dog. It was with this in mind that some theologians and philosophers, such as Ward,[16] have claimed that God created the world in order to have something to love, otherwise he would be self-sufficient and egoistical. But the one necessary being could not give himself wholly to a finite person, and so there would be still be something egoistical left over. There is only solution that resolves the dilemma: that the one necessary person is a One that is a essentially a co-equal and co-eternal First and Second, and a First and Second that are likewise One, each giving himself fully to the other. Therefore, in the terminology of Christian Trinitarianism, The First and The Second will be two hypostases in one substance, one Being eternally self-differentiating into two co-equal personal centres. In this way, the one necessary being, in being the archetype of personhood and thus of persons in relation, would be also the archetype of community in which everything that each is and has is eternally shared by the other—whereas with us, for one reason or another, there is always something which we cannot fully share.[17] Yes, the existence of anything else apart from God is "superfluous," as Ward says it would be if God did not need it as something to love, but it is so in its original sense of "overflowing," the overflowing love that is God. As Ward rightly says, the Christian message is that God *is* love; so, contrary to what Ward concludes, he must be love essentially and not secondarily as a result of what he has created.[18] Whether one could show that the one necessary being must also be Three, as Christian theology affirms and some philosophers have tried to prove *a priori*, I do not know.[19] But the one necessary being cannot be an Aristotelian God, confined to himself and his own thinking about thinking, and must in some way be a community of at least One in Two and Two in One.

6. The One Necessary Being and God

Having shown that there can be only one necessary being, and that its attributes must be fully integrated, we have since referred to it as the one necessary being. We have also shown that the one necessary being is personal, and not only personal but the exemplar of personhood and of personhood in relation or community, One in at least Two. The question now arises, Is the one necessary being God?

I have deliberately refrained from using "God" of the one necessary being, not because of any personal hesitation about theism but for the contrary reason, that "God" has been too loosely used in European philosophy and thought generally and thus has been applied to conceptions of entities unworthy of the name. Yet it should be clear by now that what has been demonstrated about the one necessary being coincides with what theism maintains about God: that he is the one necessary being, eternal, whole, perfect, personal and the archetype of personal existence. But there is at least one attribute of God that cannot be abstractly demonstrated: holiness. Here is one of the limits of "pure reason alone"; it cannot demonstrate that a subject has those attributes which, in order to know them, we have to experience at first hand and *en personne* in encountering the subject in question. For example, no *arguments* can prove that something is beautiful. No description of a painting or a woman can convey its or her beauty, only the sight of the subject itself or herself, or another painting or photograph of her (a poem can intimate something but not the precise beauty in question). This is true also of elegance, charm, and graciousness and, indeed, their contraries. For this knowledge is not a mere "knowing about" that can be passed on at second-hand, as most of our factual knowledge is, but is essentially a *responsive* knowing, a knowing that incorporates admiration. This is even more so with holiness. To know God is to be moved to adore, trust, and obey him and that cannot be reduced simply to any mere "knowing about" that could be encapsulated in a set of propositions, but not even to knowing at all. It is a knowledge that surpasses knowledge, as does the knowledge of moral values and qualities, to know which is to be drawn to them and to desire to cherish, conserve, and enhance them and their bearers. To call the one necessary being "God" is therefore to go beyond mere knowing about him, beyond philosophy as it is understood these days.

But what is God? When Aquinas asked this question, he answered, "Being." God is "He Who Is"—the one, necessarily existent, eternal, omniscient, and omnipotent being. But "being" by itself is indistinguishable from nothing. Against the "blank unity" often attributed to the one necessary being, God, the Absolute or Brahman, it was argued in Ch. 3 §3 and again in §4 of this chapter that the one necessary being must be a self-differentiating unity, neither one without distinctions nor a unity of mere parts. Is it possible to suggest what is the ultimate, comprehensive, and self-differentiating unity of all of these attributes? Christianity has a clear answer: "God is love,"[20] though even eminent theologians sometimes appear not fully to have appreciated its full significance. Can a natural theology converge upon that answer? I think to some extent it can. For example, following Max Scheler, and contrary to the usual assumption that love, along with emotions and desires, depends upon acts of cognition, it can be shown that cognition is a function of love, such that without a prior taking-an-interest-in or loving attitude to reality in general and specific regions of it, we would not know anything.[21] Again, it can be shown that all the virtues are specifications of love (*agapé*, *caritas*)—love of the right and good; that love is itself what is ultimately loved, and so is the way and the goal; and that each person is a unique stream of love or is distorted in hatred and diminished in apathy.[22] To summarise, let alone to expand these accounts is far beyond the scope of this study. In any case, all of them have themselves been inspired by Christian theology and so are not the products of unaided human reasoning upon experience. For what follows, it will be sufficient to have shown that God is self-giving love, whether or not that includes all his other attributes and powers.

Notes

1. E.g., Findlay, *Ascent to the Absolute*, 253.
2. See J. A. Passmore, *Philosophical Reasoning*, Ch. 2.
3. *The Tacit Dimension*, 34ff; see also the later essays in *Knowing and Being* and in Pt IV of *Society, Economics and Philosophy*.
4. Strawson argues that a world of sound would not give anyone in it any concept of, or means of identifying, "objective particulars," but only recurrences of the same sort or pattern of sound, and so physical objects are "basic" (necessary preconditions) for identifying objective particulars, and hence minds or persons: identifying individual minds is possible only if they are embodied (*Individuals*, 66-84). But in doing so, he begs the question by including in his world of sound only mere sounds and never voices which could, as on the wireless, identify and re-identify themselves. They would also provide, which Strawson says would be impossible, a public for identifying "public" sounds, that is, mere sounds.
5. See *Personal Knowledge*, passim.

6.   See, for example, *Formalism in Ethics*, 372-3, 384.
7.   The *Principle of Individuality and Value*, 272, 287-8, 314, 323, 325, 373; *The Value and Destiny of the Individual*, 52, 59; *The Psychology of the Moral Self;* and "On the General Will" (in *Science and Philosophy*).
8.   Polanyi, *Personal Knowledge*, Ch. 6, "Intellectual Passions," Ch. 4, "Skills," and 275-7.
9.   There is a large literature on the claims of AI: for a convenient summary, see G.D. Martin, *Does it Matter?*, Chs. 2 and 3.
10. See below, Ch. 5 §3, on God and choice in relation to a finite world.
11. On values as inhering only in a person and supremely in God, see also Sorley, *Moral Values and the Idea of God*, esp. Ch. V, and, on Lotze and C.C.J. Webb, see Bengtsson, *The Worldview of Personalism*, 201-2, 269.
12. For example, Bradley, *Appearance and Reality*, 363.
13. On this error, and also on what follows regarding the "reformist" fallacy, and for a detailed account of the logical relations of all value terms, moral and non-moral, see my *The Structure of Value*, Ch. 2.
14. A modified form of this error is again to be found in Bradley, *Ethical Studies*, 232-50, in which, though a genuinely positive side to morality is acknowledged, morality is identified with *moralisation, becoming* moral, rather than with *being* moral, and hence always needing the non-moral and the immoral to be turned into the moral.
15. For example, God in Kant's *Religion within the Bounds of Pure Reason Alone*, is solely the Judge who assess the moral worth of human conduct and never a loving Father who looks forwards to what they could and should be and inspires and helps them to attain it. Grace, in Kant's eyes, is indulgence, as if human parents should never teach or help their children but leave them entirely to their own devices, for only what a man does *by himself* has moral worth (40).
16. *Rational Theology*, 81-7, 137-8.
17. See, A.E. Taylor, *The Faith of a Moralist*, Vol. 1, 246-50. Ward rejects Trinitarianism as entailing three gods but does not mention the doctrine of the complete circumintercession (mutual indwelling) of the Three Persons. For a detailed and illuminating account of the reciprocal increase in inner diversity with self-determination and outer communication with communion (as one ascends from sub-atomic particles through the levels of inanimate, animate, conscious, and self-conscious existence, until one passes beyond all finite existence to God) see *Love and The Person* by J. Cowburn, SJ. And for more on the development of the idea of the personality *of* God as more than the traditional idea of personality *in* God, the "dialogical" conception of persons, and the consequent "social" conception of the Trinity, see Bengtsson, *Worldview*, especially Ch. 3 and references to Jacobi, Lotze, J.R.R. Illingworth and C.C.J. Webb.
18. *Rational Theology*, 85, 138.
19. For details of such speculations by Plotinus, Pseudo-Dionysius, Eriugena, Cusanus, Leibniz and Hegel, and the author's own, see J. Macquarrie, *In Search of Deity*. For the most part these Trinitarian speculations refer to merely logical relations and not to personal being.
20. 1 Jn 4:8.
21. "*Liebe und Erkenntnis.*" See also my "The cognitive functions of emotion," (*Appraisal*, Vol. 3 No. 1, March 2000, 38-47; *Polanyiana*, Vol. 15, No.s 1-2, 2006, 21-40), which draws also upon Polanyi and Macmurray. Scheler starts with love but then writes about "taking an interest in," which may not be quite same as fully developed love. Certainly, by "taking an interest in" Scheler means

a primarily disinterested attitude, and not one confined to what is necessary for merely biological processes which would carve out an "environment" and not an open "world"—the totality of existence as opposed to that which is relevant only to life-processes or any other limited interest. Such an interest in things for their own sakes is an incipient love and, we may presume, it will become such unless it is stunted and turns into limited interests and then into apathy or is perverted into hatred. Indeed, in the great reductionisms of the modern age we see such perversions. They are surely motivated by hatred of those realms and levels of existence which they try to identify with, or to explain in terms of, lower levels.

22.   See Scheler, *The Nature of Sympathy and Formalism in Ethics*. Scheler, in these works and others from 1911 to 1923, owed much to Augustine. For a detailed treatment of Augustine's writings on love, see Burnaby, *Amor Dei*.

5

The Relation of the Necessary God to a Merely Possible World

1. Cosmism and Acosmism

From God, the one necessary being, we turn to his relation to whatever else may exist, which can be only finite and merely possible realities. This is no mere addendum to the previous enquiries, because God, as the one necessary being, is now the only candidate for the role of the Absolute, as explained at the end of Chapter 2. His existence explains itself, but how does it explain everything else? Some sketch, at least, of an answer should be provided. Moreover, it has frequently been argued that the existence of a finite world reflects back upon the nature of God in very significant ways, and such arguments cannot be completely ignored here. In tackling these questions, we shall still take a primarily non-empirical approach and consider the relation of God to *any* world, and hence to the formal attributes of merely possible and finite existence as such. Any specific features of this world will be used, as before, only to illustrate the problems and solutions.

It will be convenient first to review the principal forms of cosmology which, in one way or another, deny or compromise the necessity of God or the merely possible status of everything else, or both. They are that the one or the other does not exist ("cosmism" or "acomism"); that they are identical or that God is within the world but not identical with it ("pantheism" or "immanentism"); or that God, although remaining infinite, is nevertheless made finite to some extent by the existence of the world. The last we shall examine in the next chapter for it accepts much of the account of God as the creator of this and any world which will be provided below in answer to the other problems raised and solutions proposed.

Firstly, consider cosmism and acosmism. The former holds that only the universe exists and can take two principal forms: (a) that which affirms that the universe has a merely possible existence; and (b) that which explicitly or implicitly holds the universe, its structure, and sometimes everything within to exist or happen necessarily. The latter we shall consider with "immanentist" cosmologies, which bring God, or some aspects of God, within the universe. As for the former, we can dismiss it straight away for something necessary must exist and it has been proved to be God.

As for acosmism, that only the one necessary being exists, it may appear that it is so contrary to our basic convictions about the world that we can similarly rule it out at the start. But it requires consideration because of the distinguished thinkers who have maintained it, especially those of the school of Advaita (Non-Dualist) Vedanta—of whom we shall take Shankara as the representative. How can he possibly explain away the reality of the world and us with it? Parmenides, on one interpretation, appears simply to have dismissed it as the non-thought of what is not, but Shankara rightly felt obliged to give an explanation of it. For that purpose he uses the idea of "sublation" (*badha*) whereby in a later experience a previous one is seen to have been illusory—as in the stock example of a rope originally mistaken for a snake but now seen to be the rope that it is or when in waking consciousness we realise that the contents of a dream were unreal. As the illusion of a snake is now seen to have been "superimposed" upon the rope, so the world is *maya* ("appearance," "illusion"), the product of "ignorance" (*avidya*), and is superimposed upon Brahman, the sole reality. When, by study of the Vedas, and especially the Upanishads, one comes to experience for oneself the mystical insight revealed and recorded in them that Brahman is the Self (or Essence) of oneself and all other things, then ignorance vanishes and with it everything else save Brahman. The whole phenomenal world is sublated by this experience in which nothing is superimposed upon Brahman itself, pure and eternal. But illusion presupposes two realities: the event of the illusion itself and the person who experiences it. A dream is a real event, even though the events in it do not really happen, and there can be no dream without a dreamer. It is not the dream as an event that is sublated but only its reference to reality. Similarly, this is the case with perceptual illusions. If I think that I see someone walking past the window, then that thought is a real event and I exist to think it, even though no one at that time did pass by the window. So, if the whole phenomenal world and every finite person in it is to be sublated like a dream, then *whose* illusion was it or *whose* ignorance caused it to happen? Certainly not Brahman's, for from Brahman's point of view there is, was, and ever will be only Brahman. Shankara's way out of this dilemma is to say that the world is neither existent nor non-existent.[1] But surely this is simply to dodge the problem. While he denies it any existence at all, he must still admit the patent fact that it does exist as an event (in *whose* experience?) otherwise he himself would not be there to argue against those who assert its existence in the former manner.[2]

The denial of one's own existence is even more problematical. *I* cannot coherently say that I do not exist nor that I neither exist nor do not exist. Shankara must exist in order to be deluded into thinking that he does exist—as St. Augustine said, *"si fallor, sum"* (though I err, yet I am)—and to see through his ignorance in thinking that he exists. Shankara is aware of this problem and appears to accept the *cogito*: "For every one is conscious of the existence of (his) Self, and never thinks "I am not."[3] This starts with "I," as referring to the individual, finite self but "his Self" is not his individual self but Brahman, the Self, the essence of and true reality behind all phenomenal objects on which, in ignorance, they are superimposed. Thus he starts with what looks as if it is going to be "I, Shankara, am" but ends, in effect, with "I, Brahman (the Self), am." What we expect to take as the very affirmation of the individual's own existence is turned into its denial. But that is the whole problem: How can I coherently deny that I do not exist but am the product of ignorance (*whose*?) and a superimposition (by *whom*?) upon Brahman? Any radical acosmism cannot be coherently stated. Whether or not there was when only the one necessary being existed or will be when only it will exist, assuredly some other things now also exist, ourselves among them, and the question of how they are related to it necessarily arises.

Nevertheless, it may be objected that the above is a set of *a posteriori* arguments against the coherence of acosmism, to the effect that we cannot coherently deny that there is a finite world in which we exist as finite beings. In contrast, what *this* study really requires is something quite different; namely, an *a priori* argument to show that acosmism would be incoherent irrespective of the existence of any finite beings. That would be to prove *a priori* that it is coherent to think of God as the origin of the existence of finite beings. Then, because God can be the creator of all finite being, as the one necessary being he must be able to be their cause or origin. For the present, let us consider immanentist cosmologies which unite the necessary one and the merely possible many. One common argument for them is that the co-existence of the infinite (the one necessary being) and the finite finitises the former. If we can prove that this is false and that, in contrast, the one necessary being can be the cause of finite beings, then we shall also have disproved acosmism *a priori*.

2. Pantheisms and Immanentisms

Immanentist cosmologies attempt to unite the one necessary being with the merely possible many while retaining in some way both necessary being from the former and finite existence from the latter. Necessarily, though it is usually assumed by default, immanentist cosmologies hold there to be only one world which includes all merely possible beings—though conceivably an immanentist cosmology could envision more than one provided they were not wholly separate. Examples of immanentist cosmologies are:

1.   Spinoza's, in which finite beings are "modes" of the one substance, God or Nature, which is throughout a necessary system.
2.   Blanshard's, in which the universe is a necessary system comprising finite elements.[4]
3.   Bradley's, in which finite beings are "appearances" of the non-relational Absolute that, however, can exist only in and through its appearances (unlike Brahman in Advaita Vedantism).
4.   Hegel's, in which the Idea either (a) creates and embodies itself in the world in order to find and return to itself or (b) is the necessary system of categories that is the framework of the world and of historical development, but which also needs contingency (mere possibility) of detail.
5.   "Emergent" cosmologies, in which God or the one necessary being comes into existence in the world and as its consummation—e.g., those of the later Max Scheler, Samuel Alexander and E.E. Harris.[5]

We cannot properly investigate the details and logic of each of them here and can only examine the more general problems that arise from conflating the one necessary being and the many.

Firstly, those systems which would explain all events in the universe solely by reference to necessary laws face the problem that all laws are formal and hypothetical and require a "matter" which they cannot supply in order to be categorical. For example, on a planet with no liquids there is nothing to which the laws of hydrodynamics can apply. On lifeless planets, there is nothing to instantiate biological evolution and natural selection. If no other planets existed, those laws would not apply at all. Even if the laws of the universe are ontologically and unconditionally necessary, and no one has yet shown that they are, then they do not by themselves create the "matter," let alone in any particular amount, which would be required for them actually to apply to something. For example, it would have to be a necessary fact that there are only *n* elements in the universe, and those in certain amounts and relative proportions. "Matter" is an ingredient of pre-eminent mere possibility. Whatever our system of natural science, and whatever the universe may be, something has to be taken as merely given and hence as non-necessary.[6]

In addition some laws refer to, and some structural features of the world consist of, specific constants or ratios: e.g., $e = mc^2$, Planck's constant $h = 6.62559$ percent 10^{-34} joule seconds, the actual speed of light, the actual rate of acceleration due to gravity. As we saw in Ch. 3 §2, quantity entails finitude and hence non-necessity, as also do all variable attributes, space and situations. I do not doubt that the universe would be very different if even one of these fundamental constants or ratios were other than it happens to be. But that is the whole point: it is not logically and ontologically necessary that it be what it in fact is, and the same would apply to any physical universe. And in any case laws cannot *do* anything but describe the ways in which the universe does regularly operate. It is a gross fallacy to reify laws into agents.

There cannot be multiple necessary beings, and hence if the laws of the universe are to be unconditionally necessary, then they must be strictly be reducible to *one* law, a genuine "theory of everything." But one can claim to envisage such a theory only by a reductionism that simply omits the vast variety and complexity of the universe. Above all, any such reductionism and any determinism whatsoever comes up against what no one can deny in his own case—the *cogito* and self-responsibility. No one who professes universal determinism actually believes it, for he always tacitly exempts himself from its sway. In his own experience, he knows that he is the source of his acts, that what he does is primarily what he decides to do. Even those who say that determinism is required so that *we* can effectively influence the behaviour of others reveal not only their essentially manipulative attitude towards their fellows, but implicitly ascribe to themselves, or to an unspecified "us," the power to *decide* what they or we want others to be. They tacitly view themselves as the unconditioned conditioners of others.[7] Those who, like Blanshard, regard freedom as the conscious following of the necessities of logic, such as the choice of the greatest good at hand, incur the problem of the interventions of the physical and mental orders upon each other, which makes their joint outcome merely possible. The presence of some of the elements in my situation is not rationally, but only causally necessary; hence they are a merely possible "matter" for my choice (even if, as is not the case, there is always one greatest good) and conversely the effects of my choice, entail a break with the antecedent chain of physical causation which would have continued otherwise had I not acted at all. Thus, this is a merely possible "matter" for the relevant causal laws. The only way to save necessity is to eliminate the one order in favour of the other: either materialism and causation or monistic mentalism and a universal rational mind operating through all minds. In any case, logical rationalism cannot account for the manifest actuality of innumerable irrational choices.

At least one sphere of existence exhibits what Hayek has called "predictions in principle"; that is, ones which cannot be precisely formulated at all but of which we can say only that something like *A* or *B* is likely to happen. That sphere is life and the evolution of life into its manifold forms. The whole point of the modern meaning of evolution is that something new emerges from a previous form (the older meaning was that the new was already there in germ or embryo, like the plant "evolving" from the seed). Precisely because it is a new form, and not just an additional instance of an existing one, it cannot be predicted from nor explained in terms of what already exists. If it could, it would be only a reduplication of it. Darwinism and Neo-Darwinism, contrary to what is often said, do not provide explanations of evolution—that is, of the *emergence* of the new, but only of the *survival* or *extinction* of forms that already exist. As for the emergence of new forms, that is explained by random genetic variation. But "random" means that the variation or mutation of genes *cannot* be explained: it is the acknowledgement that such mutation simply happens and for no rhyme or reason. Evolution on the grand scale, of life from the lifeless, of complex from simple organisms, of sentient from non-sentient ones, and then of self-conscious and self-responsibility with man, increases the gap between the existing and the new, and the impossibility of explaining the emergence of the new in terms of the laws that explain the operations of the existing. For what emerges are new forms with new laws and operational principles of their own.[8] Hence they cannot be necessitated by what already exists and so must be merely possible. Of course, explanations have been offered of how new forms come into being from what already exists, but they end up either preserving the newness of the new and so simply restating what is to be explained, or closing the gap and so denying the newness of the new.[9]

This raises the whole question of time. If there could be a static universe, it could seem (but to *whom*?) to exist necessarily and necessarily to exist in the way that it does. But temporality manifests mere possibility, because what now exists and happens once did not exist or happen. The actual is clearly possible, otherwise it could not be actual, but that which comes into and goes out of existence is only possible and not necessary. Hence the tendency for immanentist systems to deny the reality of time, or to reduce the world to regular movements of a constant number of atoms in which nothing truly new ever occurs, or to regard the universe as moving through an ever recurring series of cycles. The problem with all denials of the reality of time is that we do not merely observe time but are immersed in it. McTaggart, to his credit, did not simply argue against the reality of time, but also offered an "error theory" to explain how we come to think that it is real: namely, that we mistake logical relations of "included in" and "inclusive of" for temporal sequences of earlier and later, respectively. But this refutes itself, because it entails a genuine temporal sequence of being mistaken about time and then coming to a correct view, a real change in us, especially in the final stage when "apparent time," our present experience, has fallen away. And if *that* sequence is taken to be a logical one mistaken for a temporal one, then the same problem returns when we realise that error. If time were unreal, then we ourselves would have to be unchanging and hence be always in error or always correct. As for cyclical cosmologies, they now have to deny the Second Law of Thermodynamics with its consequences of universal entropy and "heat death" in the future, and all the evidence pointing to "Big Bang" in the past. Nothing, in this world, has lasted or will last forever.

Hegel saw that some amount of contingency (mere possibility) is necessary to any actual world; at a given point, *something* of sort A is seen to be necessary but not any particular a_1, a_2, a_3, etc. That, for Hegel, renders it not so merely possible after all. But does his dialectical expansion of concepts show that the structural framework of the universe and the main lines of historical development are necessary? I do not think that it does or can and that his dialectic is made to prove the necessity of whatever Hegel finds to come next, just as Marxist theoreticians purported to show, after each event, that their master's materialist dialectics had all along predicted it.

These problems obviously arise only in worlds which are substantially like ours and have causal orders, living beings and conscious ones, and are temporal. If a totally inert and "frozen" world were possible, they would not apply to it. Yet even then that of the allegedly necessary existence of finite beings would still arise, and with it the general problem of "singularity": just why do *these* sorts of things exist and in the species, amounts, extents, and numbers that they do? To this, no answers in terms of necessity can be given. Finite and merely possible reality cannot include or be included in the one necessary being.

3. The Dualism of the One Necessary Being and the Merely Possible Many

The reality of neither the one necessary being nor the cosmos can be denied, and neither can the one necessary being be coherently brought down into or identified with the cosmos, nor the cosmos elevated to the status of the one necessary being or absorbed into it. Consequently, we are left with only one other possibility: some sort of dualism in which both are real and distinct. Yet any such dualism has been held to be incoherent. One argument against it, given by Passmore, is that "being" or "existence" is either univocal when applied to any two worlds or different orders of existence, so that they then can be said only to have the same sort of being or existence and not two different ones, or that these terms are equivocal and so of one of them nothing is being said about its being or existence.[10] This simply omits the possibility of the analogical uses of words and betrays complete ignorance of etymology. Passmore also claims that "cause" as used of God in relation to the world becomes emptied of meaning as it is denied that there is no precedence in time, no change in agent, and so on. He requires theologians to spell out their analogies and implies that nothing is left if they do so.[11] But we can easily state what remains when "cause" is applied to God—"bringing something about," which is the root meaning of "cause." Indeed, God's causality is "eminent" and that of finite beings deficient, for, as we shall see, he primarily brings creatures into existence *ex nihil* and not by changing things that already exists. Our imaginations can be creative in regard to thoughts and produce ideas which have never been thought before, but for real existence in the world, we can cause *A* to exist only by modifying some already existent *B* or by setting in motion some already existing process, such as human reproduction. Likewise, this applies to the existence of different orders or levels of entities. Not all physical objects exist in exactly the same way; flames, rivers, and organisms persist even though their physical constituents are continuously replacing each other. On the human level, modes of existence and their interrelations can vary even more. Not only do organisations persist independently of the successions of their "matter"—the persons who belong to them and pass through them—but they can change location, be suspended and revived, dissolved and re-established, abolished and restored. Indeed, an office can continue to exist even when unfilled, such as the living of parish in the Church of England during an interregnum, or the monarchy in Hungary when there was no king at all. The same unit of money can exist in several physical forms, and, as well as that in which it is embodied, money exists today primarily as believed to exist and thus will cease to exist as money, though not physically, when declared not to be legal tender, as with Confederate dollars, Tsarist roubles, the Brazilian real, and now French and Belgian francs. Consequently, there can be no objection in principle to even more radically different modes of existence—such as that of the one necessary being and the merely possible many.

A second claim, as made by Passmore and Edward Caird whom he quotes, is that there can be no interaction across such a radical ontological gap as that between the eternal and spiritual God and the temporal and physical world; a thesis that has already been rejected in respect of mind and body.[12] As well as our general answer to that contention, there is also one specific to the present question which we shall soon be able to make: that God, as the creator of all finite existence, does not find any physical matter with fixed qualities and powers already in existence but brings it into existence and gives it the qualities and powers that he determines. The universe can respond to God because he has made it. Nor is this a "dogmatic" reply. For, as we shall see in the section after the next, creation is the only way that the necessary One and the unnecessary many can be related without destroying the integrity of each.

Finally, combining the assumption that language is either univocal or equivocal with the claim that the co-existence of God and the world must finitise God, Passmore, this time citing Tillich, argues that a duality of the world and God would place a supernatural world alongside the natural, fixing a beginning and end to God's creativity, and making God a cause like other causes and an individual substance like other such substances.[13] Tillich's solution was to make God simply an otherwise empty "Ground of Being." His mistake was, yet again, to begin by imagining God and the world as existing side by side. So too did Hegel, who, though not wholly denying the reality of the merely possible, nevertheless was opposed to the separation of necessary being (the "true infinite") and merely possible being (the finite). Rightly rejecting the idea of pure being as a blank or empty being but yet holding implicitly to the Cusan thesis that all determination is negation, he dialectically unfolds the concept of being and thus also that of nothingness, its equally blank and thus indistinguishable opposite, as achieving reality by their union in becoming, determinate being.[14] In light of this, he later unites the infinite with the finite and explicitly rejects any dualism of the infinite and the finite because, placing them alongside each other, must finitise both.[15] But this is itself based on that picture-thinking which Hegel was only too ready, as here, to impute to others, and especially to "the religious consciousness." He not only expounds what is involved in imagining the infinite and the finite; God and the cosmos, as *situated* over and against each other and thus as finite; but is himself using this same crude picture-thinking in order to interpret and condemn any cosmological distinction of the one God and the many finite beings. Therefore, he simply does not consider any other formulation of such a cosmology. It is, ultimately, on the same level as those refutations of theism which do nothing but poke fun at the image of an old man with a beard in the sky. If God and the cosmos were simply situated over and against each other then we would have the contradictions involved in conceiving of two necessary beings. But the dualism of God and the cosmos (or cosmoi) is not one of two entities of the same category or status and in the same "logical space," but of two categories of being, of the one of which there can be only one instance.

The cosmos (or cosmoi) cannot exist apart from God for it is merely possible, nor *alongside* God, nor be incorporated within God, nor incorporate God within itself, either "from the beginning" or at the end as in the emergentist cosmologies mentioned above. Therefore, we must seek for another relation between them, which can be only that of the real but dependent existence of the cosmos upon God. The cosmos cannot exist independently of God, nor as in some way one with God. Hence, it can have only a dependent independence. It must have substantive existence and cannot be an "adjective," aspect or part of God which would make it necessary and not merely possible; yet it cannot exist by itself, for then again it would be necessary and not merely possible, and so it must exist not only as distinct from God but also as dependent upon and sustained by God.

Can we further specify this relationship? There are at least two ways in which its been conceived: as "emanation" by Neo-Platonism and as creation by theism. We shall now examine them to discover if either, or even both, has fundamental difficulties and thus if the other or some third is to be preferred.

But first let us note that we have now completed the task set at the end of §1 above. We now have shown *a priori* that it is coherent to think of God as the cause or origin of the existence of the many merely possible beings, and hence that God must be their cause or origin if they exist. Consequently, we have proved *a priori*, and quite apart from the actual existence of any finite world at all, that acosmism is false in holding that the one necessary being could not be the cause of, nor even co-exist with, any finite beings.

5. Emanation and Creation

According to Plotinus, every order of being necessarily emanates something other than itself, which carries something of its own essence but without diminishing itself and which is less than, and so inferior to, the former.[16] Certainly for everything below the One, the supreme existent, this is a necessary principle, and so *Nous*, the Divine Mind contemplating the Platonic Forms, emanates the Soul, the third divine principle, which in turn emanates the world in which each higher order emanates a lower. But as to the first emanation, of *Nous* by the One, it is both described in the same words as other emanations yet does not entail any external "necessity" but is a "part" of the One's self-willing of himself.[17] Nevertheless, because the One does not concern itself with *Nous*, *a fortiori* Soul, and the world, their existence seems not truly to be willed but to be more like an unintended and unnoticed, and therefore inadvertent, consequence of the One's willing of himself. The reason for the attribution to the One of a lack of concern for anything beyond itself, is Plotinus' insistence on the radical otherness of the One, its infinity and lack of all division and duality, which makes it difficult for him to say anything positive about the One's knowledge, even of himself which would introduce into him a distinction between subject and object.[18] Yet if the One truly "makes" the Forms, Matter and so on, surely he must know what he is doing and do it deliberately? It is ironic that Plotinus, trying so hard to avoid any suspicion of finitude in the One, should apparently deny him knowledge of his own activity and make it seem either that the One unintentionally sets off the process of emanation or that it is a cosmic law prior to and independent of him, just as it is in relation to all finite beings.

A further problem with emanation is that it is the same process that generates *Nous*, the Divine Mind which includes and contemplates the Forms, and then Soul in turn. *Nous* and Soul are eternal though with finite aspects. But can it be *exactly* the same process that crosses the radical gaps (a) between the wholly infinite One and the infinite-finite *Nous* and Soul, (b) between the last and wholly finite beings, and (c) between two such wholly finite existences as fire and the heat that it radiates (Plotinus' model for emanation)? Finally, emanation can apply only to a world that cascades down from the fullness of being in the One to its lowest possible form, even if this be construed in a logical and non-temporal sense in order to avoid the problem of higher levels, such as organic existence, emanating the lower ones, inanimate matter, upon which they depend for their existence. In neither form can it apply to one, such as ours, which began with only the lowest upon which higher levels then supervened. These problems with the idea of emanation stem from two principal sources: the implicit acceptance of the Cusanian axiom which makes it impossible for Plotinus to say little about what the One positively is, and an incompletely personalist conception of the One that leaves it unclear if emanation proceeds automatically from the One, even without his knowledge, or if it is indeed freely willed by him. As the first in European history fully to grasp and assert the transfinite nature of God, above and beyond the finite world, and as living in what was still a polytheistic *milieu*, Plotinus did not have adequate alternative conceptions at hand. The way forward lies, not in retreat from personal conceptions, but in a through-going application of them.

For no finite and merely possible world can come into existence by any sort of necessary process, for then its existence would be necessary, and, as immanentist cosmologies hold, it would in some way or other be a part of the one all-inclusive and necessarily existing Whole. Only the idea of a *personal* act of creation *ex nihil* and by sheer fiat provides the answer to the problems of relating the one necessary being to the many merely possible ones. On the one hand, it preserves the unique necessity of God. As wholly created by him, or as generated by and within a world wholly created by him, finite beings are dependent upon him for their existence and their nature. Nothing exists independently of him "from the beginning" and so nothing is *given* to him.[19] Therefore, the Creator is not one finite being existing alongside one or more others, and so is neither a merely possible being who just happens to exist and to exist with one or more others, nor an element in the one, and seemingly necessarily existent, cosmic system. On the other hand, creation, as a definite and free act of choice, and in contrast to the apparently unwilled, unconscious, and necessary emanation of a world, entails that what comes into existence is not necessary but contingent upon that choice, which could have been otherwise, both in the Creator's choice to create a world or some worlds and in the decision to create a particular world or particular worlds and not others. Any necessities in a finite world will be conditional ones contingent upon the decision of the Creator to create that world and to arrange it in that way with those laws: if *B* follows necessarily from or accompanies *A*, then this because the Creator has chosen that it should do. Some laws or arrangements could not be otherwise in any physical world or finite world whatsoever, such as the dependence of organisms upon a non-organic environment and the embodiment of minds in living bodies and not in merely physical and inanimate ones. Nevertheless it would not be the case that any such laws and arrangements would *have* to be instantiated, such that there would have to be a finite world, that it would have to be a physical world, and that it must include embodied minds.

In view of current controversies regarding "creationism" and "evolution," in which the two most vociferous parties collude in confusing the whole question by identifying "creation" with the "special creation" of each species and, even worse, of the whole universe more or less as it is now in a single act a few thousand years ago, it is appropriate here to elaborate the real meaning and implications of "creation."

It cannot mean what it did in Deism, that God made the world and then left it to run on of its own accord. The motive for this interpretation of the idea was to banish all possibility of God's intervention in the world by way specific acts of revelation (or "special revelation" as it is sometimes called), inspiration, miracles, "special providences" (that is, acts not obviously contrary to the usual course of things) signs, and so on; everything upon which an historical religion depends and which gives it its authority. But, because only the Creator exists necessarily, all finite being depends upon his will, not just for its origin, but also for its continued existence. It can continue to exist and to run in its usual course only insofar as God wills it so to do. Whatever it does, he has total control over it.

The idea of creation as a personal activity therefore leaves open the possibility of those things which Deism detested. A natural theology may be able, by analogies with human activity, to suggest that the Creator is likely directly to "intervene," that is, to conduct the processes of some part of the universe in a way different from their usual course, directly to manifest himself in and through particular events and persons, and even to appear *en personne* in a creaturely form. But only an historical theology can indicate if, when, where, and how he has definitely done so.

The idea of creation also leaves open the manner of how and when the Creator brings finite beings into existence: e.g., all at once or over a longer or shorter spell of time; directly ("special creation") or indirectly via other finite beings to which he has given the power to remould each other (as the movements of the earth's tectonic plates open up trenches and rift valleys, push up mountains, and cause earthquakes) to reproduce themselves, perhaps with changes which amount to new species (that is, the creation of new species by evolution from existing ones) or to make and invent new things. Whatever happens and however it happens, it is because he has created things to do what they do and in the way that they do. Again, only an empirical study of what happens and has happened can tell us in each case what he has done.

From the idea of creation as God's relation to any finite being, certain attributes of God that are traditional in theism immediately follow: omniscience, omnipresence, and omnipotence.

God is primarily not a detached observer of a world set over and against himself, who has to wait and see what will happen or infer what will happen from what evidence there is at hand, but is its creator—the world is, and operates, as he has decided that it should. His knowledge of it, therefore, is that form of knowing that every agent has of what he is doing in the doing of it. But whereas finite agents have to cope with situations which they have not created and so often cannot know what their actions will amount to, God creates everything that he deals with and so knows what it is and what it will do. Again, because we are finite and created, we depend upon limited and fallible mental and physical powers, so that we can be confused and forgetful about what we are doing and attempt things beyond our powers. But God, the creator of everything else, does not depend upon and so is not limited by anything else. God necessarily knows what he is doing and hence what is happening in the world even when *what* he knows is merely possible.

Again, because God knows directly, not by inference and conjecture, what he and therefore the world is doing, he is omnipresent, not so much *in* it as if he were located within it as we are, but *to* it, just as is the writer to his novel or play. Rather, as the novel or play is open to its author, the world is omnipresent to God; it is totally open to him and nothing is hidden from him.

Finally, as the creator of all finite beings, and not the shaper of any pre-existing "matter," God is not limited in power by them but has complete control over them, as noted above, and can do whatever he pleases with them, and with anything else that he may will into existence. There is nothing, properly speaking, that he cannot do. Anything that he appears unable to do will prove to be a "non-thing," a logical impossibility, a juxtaposition of incompossible ideas—as with Euclidian triangles whose interior angles do not add up to 180 degrees and with perpetual-motion machines.

Yet claims have often been made that one or more of these attributes of God is incompatible with the existence of a finite world or some specific feature of it or, at least, must be revised so as to be compatible with it. Some of these we have already mentioned, and it is now time to deal with them.

Notes

1. Radhakrishnan and Moore, 155.
2. The same applies to "appearances" in Bradley's cosmology. For appearances can be such only by appearing, but to whom? Not to the Absolute in itself, as if it could not grasp itself as it really is, but only to other appearances. It seems to be a system only of mirrors and distorting ones at that.
3. ibid., p. 115.
4. *Reason and Analysis*, Chs. IX-XII.
5. See: Scheler, *Die Stellung des Menschen im Kosmos* (trans. as *Man's Place in the Cosmos*); Alexander, *Space, Time and Deity*; E.E. Harris, *The Restitution of Metaphysics* and previous books.
6. As Jaki emphasises throughout *The Road of Science and the Ways to God*, it is singularity, such as the uneven distribution of stars and the specific values of constants (to be mentioned again in the next paragraph) that no wholly immanentist cosmology can explain.
7. As is explicit in B. F. Skinner's *Beyond Freedom and Dignity*.
8. See Polanyi, *Personal Knowledge*, Ch. 12, on the distinctiveness and autonomy of the sphere of life, and *The Tacit Dimension*, Ch. 2, on how each successive form or level defines, by its own operational principles, the boundary conditions left open by the next lower, so that its own operational principles explain its autonomous operations while those of the lower can explain breakdowns in the higher: e.g., how events in the brain cause schizophrenia and clinical depression but cannot explain correct mental functioning. Moreover, events on higher levels can cause disruptions on lower ones, as persistent worry engenders stomach ulcers. Nor are higher levels simply limited by lower ones, but can often take or develop alternative means when the usual ones are missing or incapacitated (see *Personal Knowledge*, 337-43 on "equipotentiality"). A spectacular example is the ability of the remaining half of the human brain to take over the functions of the missing other half, and, up to the age of eight, even those of the speech centre when it has been removed, with only a little impairment of the person's abilities.
9. Examples of the former are Polanyi's, in the final chapter of *Personal Knowledge*, and Jan Smuts' *Holism and Evolution,* in which the creativeness attributed to Nature means only that it is open to the emergence of new forms within itself. As for the latter, a common explanation is in terms of "gradualness," e.g., E.E. Harris, *The Foundation of Metaphysics in Science*, 487. But if genuinely new principles do emerge, as the evidence shows that they have, then their appearance cannot be explained by existing ones. The operation of principles on a lower level can unlock or open up opportunities for the operation of principles of a higher one, as rainfall in a desert provides the conditions for seeds to grow. But that can happen only when the higher level already exists, as here in the form of the seeds of living plants, and no purely physical principles can explain the rise of life in the first place. To say, with Harris, that "the novelty is a continuous outgrowth from the foregoing phrase" is either merely to say that it informs or organises the same "matter" (mass-energy) which is true but irrelevant, or to imply that the emergence of the new happens in sequences of small steps and hence that there is no radical break. But at the end of each sequence either something radically new has emerged or it hasn't, and something new must emerge in each step. No accumulation of

non-novelties can add up to any degree of novelty. Collingwood, in the Conclusion to the 1934 version of the lectures on Nature and Mind (*The Principles of History*, 256-7) and Harris (*Restitution of Metaphysics,* 99, 230) invoke a "nisus" on all levels to explain the emergence of higher levels. But such an explanation either ascribes characteristics of life and mind, such as directedness and intention, to the merely physical level that existed prior to their appearance and so upgrades that level to what is supposed to have emerged from it (cf. Harris, *Atheism*, 56, 65) or is a mere *vis dormativa* explanation that simply restates the fact of emergence as its own explanation. The same applies to Bergson's *élan vital*. See also Hans Jonas' immanentist emergent cosmology, as set out in *The Phenomenon of Life: Toward a Philosophical Biology* which postulates Being as developing itself from matter, through life, and mind to self-consciousness and responsibility in man. The failure of secularist attempts to explain emergence suggests an *a posteriori* argument to the existence of a fully transcendent originator and director of emergence.

10. *Philosophical Reasoning*, 39.
11. ibid., 50.
12. ibid., 48, citing *The Evolution of Theology in the Greek Philosophers* ,Vol. II, 11. See above Ch. 2, §2 (1).
13. ibid., 49, citing *Systematic Theology*, 6.
14. *Shorter Logic*, Ch. VII.
15. ibid., §95. See also E.E. Harris, *Atheism*, 84: the true infinite must be all-inclusive, for, if it excluded anything, it would then be finite.
16. *Enneads*, 5.4.2; see also 5.1.6.
17. *Enneads*, 5.1.6.18. See also the discussion by Rist, *Plotinus: The Road to Reality*, Ch. 6, and 26-7, referring to *Enneads* 4.8.6, 5.3.17, and 6.8.19. The last, says Rist, is especially significant for there Plotinus says that when the One "made" being, it was not merely "in accordance with his being," that is, not a necessary act.
18. ibid., Ch. 4.
19. E.S. Brightman, in order to account for the existence of otherwise inexplicable evils in the world (his wife died at an early age from cancer) and for mathematical, logical, and moral norms, and other Platonic forms, argued for a "Given," not set outside and before God (as with Plato) but found within God, and thus that God is finite as well as infinite (*The Problem of God, A Philosophy of Religion*). But this is surely a distinction without a difference because both the external and the internal Given are given to God and not created by him. Hence it appears, they must necessarily exist, and so the Given and God must form one system (perhaps a recognition of this lies behind the idea of an internal Given). But the recalcitrance to God of some of the Given, the obstacles it presents to him, and even conflicts within him, by which Brightman attempts to account for "surd evil" and the apparent limitations on God's power, contradict the intimate unity of necessary being, and so either neither is necessary or the one is necessary and the other merely possible and dependent on it.

6

God as Necessary but Also Finite

1. Introduction

We shall now consider those problems that have been said to arise from the conjunction of the necessary and transfinite nature of God and the existence of a created, merely possible, and finite world, and for which the solutions proposed consider God to be in some respects temporal, limited in power and knowledge, contingent, and thus finite. Hence these problems are especially relevant to this study because they seem to require a revision of the necessity of all God's attributes, as traditional theism has maintained but which, it is claimed, is not wholly sustainable. It will be argued that most of these problems arise from the use of principles which are merely meta-logical, and therefore purely abstract and unadapted to any concrete reality, or are merely meta-*physical,* and therefore inappropriate to personal existence. Consequently, they can be resolved by resolutely thinking of God in wholly personal terms appropriate to the one necessary and transfinite being. Four principles in particular will resolve most of the problems raised: that what is right and good is a sufficient but non-necessarly reason; that despite claims to the contrary, relations between God and the world can be real or cause changes in respect of the world but can be only "notional" and never cause changes in God; that this is so because in personal existence details on a lower level have to change in order that one's action and character on a higher level do not change; and that what are often taken be limits upon God's knowledge and power are not limits because they are "non-things," logical impossibilities consisting of incompossible ideas. We shall consider the principal problems with examples of them principally taken from Hartshorne, Ward, Swinburne, and Helm.

2. Why Would God Create Any Finite World?

In its original form, the principle of sufficient reason was taken to mean that only necessary reasons can be sufficient ones, in which case all reality would exist or happen necessarily and all reasoning about it could be logically necessary. As was argued in Ch. 3 §1, in that sense it could apply only to God as the one necessary being, and it must be reformed to allow that non-necessary reasons be sufficient in the case of the merely possible beings that constitute the rest of reality. With respect to personal existence, one clearly sufficient reason is that something is right and good. When we know that something is good or right, we need no further reasons (*ceteris paribus*) for choosing it nor any further explanation of another's choice of it. Nor is it the case that one is bound always to choose the best possibility, if there is one. For lesser values are still *values* and therefore worth the pursuit and realisation: light music and literature have their place alongside more serious works; fun and games alongside intellectual pursuits; parties alongside academic, political, and religious meetings. Hence a higher good is not always to be preferred to a lower one as rationalist systems, such as utilitarianism, demand. Indeed, persons who adopt such a principle easily fall into an attitude of being "more high-minded than thou."

This revised version of the principle of sufficient reason resolves the problem raised by some theologians, including eminently orthodox ones, that the creation of the world appears to be a motiveless and incomprehensible act,[1] and also the conclusion that the explanatory role of God (as the Absolute) is thereby diminished.[2] That a created and finite world would be good, or more good than bad, is a sufficient reason for creating one and a wholly intelligible act. This, of course, is an explanation for the existence of any finite world and of the general features of each particular one but not of its details. That I made a table because I thought it a good thing to do, does not explain how it was made and how it holds together.

Yet, there is still one obvious objection to what has been claimed about the role of God as the Absolute: the manifest existence of evil. How can any conception of the Absolute explain that, let alone one that maintains that finite beings exist because it is good, but not necessary, that they should exist? How can an omnipotent and good God allow evil to exist? Because evil does exist, it has been concluded that God is immoral or not omnipotent or non-existent. Against these objections, I have nothing to say that has not been said before, and so I shall briefly rehearse what I take to be the salient points.

Any claim that the finite world, and hence any evil in it, is unreal or mere appearance not only incurs the problems that we have already examined in Ch. 5 §2, but is monstrous in its denial of the wickedness and suffering in the world. And to separate the good creator from the finite world and the evil in it by attributing its origin to some other agent, as in Gnosticism, Manichaeism, or later Zoroastrianism would make both finite and requiring explanation by something beyond both. Likewise, to attribute the evils which are not freely willed by finite persons to a refractory "Given," would again finitise God by setting alongside or within him something else which is independent of him. Another set of specious solutions attempts to show that evil is inseparable from good, as the shadow cast by light, as that which good needs to fight or reform as thus to exist as good—such arguments we have already refuted in Ch. 4 §5. The problem can be legitimately reduced by showing that *some* evils are necessary or possible accompaniments of *some* goods. Thus, the possibility of evil intentions (and innocent errors which can have untoward consequences) is inherent in the existence of finite persons. For moral good, in the narrow sense, cannot be produced automatically but only as personally intended, and the state of *non posse peccari* can be attained only by a personal response to it—a response that could be refused. Hence, either no finite persons come into existence or with their existence comes the real possibility of moral evil. Again, if God were always to frustrate the execution of evil actions, or even of merely misguided ones, then the likely result would be even greater irresponsibility; it would not matter what we thought, felt and intended, as does happen with indulged children. Similarly, if sentient and especially responsible beings are to exist in a physical world, they require living bodies with which to engage in that world. Their embodiment entails physical vulnerability; for their sensitivity to the world, without which they could not perceive and act in it but lead only a vegetable existence, entails the possibility of physical impairment and pain. Yet animals live within only an immediate present of a short duration. But personal existence, with memory, anticipation, and imagination, entails that suffering of all types, the heartache as well as the thousand natural shocks, is not confined to that present but is magnified by being anticipated and remembered. A sudden blow is not as bad as one which one we see coming, and what makes chronic pain yet worse is the knowledge that it will continue. As far as a purely natural or philosophical theology is concerned, we may be able only to presume that the balance of good over evil is such that it is better that such a world should exist than not. Such a presumption would be greatly strengthened if it could also be shown that given the existence, power, and goodness of God our present life is a preparation for one to come in which human wickedness will be overcome, natural evils will fall away, and we shall be able to share for ever more in the unalloyed joy of the Lord.

3. Change in the World and Change in God

It is frequently argued that any change in what he has created must engender a change in God, who therefore cannot be altogether necessary, eternal, and immutable. Indeed, the very creation of any world must itself be a new act on God's part and therefore a change in him. Consequently, if God is wholly necessary, eternal, and immutable creation would have to be a timeless act and cause no change in God, and the created world would in reality be timeless and changeless, although mistakenly viewed as temporal from within.[3]

We can solve this dilemma if we recall what has already been determined, in Ch. 4 §4, about God's transcendence of the opposition between necessity and freedom. As we have seen, God freely and necessarily wills his own existence and nature because, as wholly actual and the union of value and being, it would be a "non-thing," a juxtaposition of incompossible ideas, and literally "unthinkable" for him to do anything else. Therefore it is a misleading question to ask whether God freely or necessarily creates a world or worlds. He is not jealous and his love naturally overflows into acts of creation, and so he freely expresses his love in freely creating beings other than himself. He does not need to, for he lacks nothing and so he acts under no internal compulsion as he acts under no external compulsion. Therefore his actions are not random but fully expressive of himself. Whatever he creates will be "superfluous," as Ward says, but as the result of the superfluity of the love that he is.[4]

In creating, God does not change but expresses his trans-partitive and self-differentiating nature in a new form. Likewise in caring for and directing his creatures, he remains what the Old Testament calls his "steadfast love." As was argued above in Ch. 3 §3 and Ch. 4 §5, consistency in personal existence *requires* changes in the details of what we do precisely in order still to do and be the same thing. Therefore all arguments which claim to show that God changes in relation and response to a changing world rest upon a failure to think about him in properly personal terms and to remember that, as the one necessary being, he is always everything that he could be. For example, in it is sometimes assumed that X is the sum total of all the true propositions that can be made about X.[5] Hence, if any one of these changes, then X changes. But this rests on a failure to distinguish between "real" (or "dynamic") relations, in which any change in them brings about or results from a change in at least one of their terms, and "nominal" (or "non-dynamic") ones, in which any change is a change only the relation itself. For example, to enter into the relation of employer and employee does make a difference to both parties because mutual obligations are thereby contracted. But to become the $n+x^{th}$ elector on an Electoral Register, instead of the nth because others have died, or moved in or out of the ward, makes no difference. Indeed, the difference made by in the former example may not make any real change to the parties themselves; their circumstances may be different, even very different, but their characters may well remain the same. Aquinas maintained, correctly, that all relations between God and created beings are real in the relation to the latter and only nominal in rest of God.[6] Changes in the relations between God and his creatures arise within the latter and do not change God, whose nature of love never changes. God remains "immutable," not because he cannot adapt to changing circumstances, but precisely because he can.[7]

Yet, there are two respects in which, despite these arguments, God may still thought to be temporal and mutable because of events among created beings—knowing what is happening *now* and coming to know what finite beings with some degree of self-determination will decide and the consequences of their decisions. It is these considerations that have impressed those especially concerned with the personal nature of God.[8] Nevertheless, they give us no reason to conclude that God is in any temporally finite.

Following Boethius and Aquinas, it has usually been held that God, being eternal and so immutable, knows everything in one all-comprehensive act, a *nunc stans*, in which there is no change.[9] Aquinas illustrates this by the analogy of a traveller on a road who can see only what is ahead of him and not those following behind him, whereas a man on a nearby hill can see at the same time both what is on the road ahead of the traveller and what is behind him.[10] This traditional account has been further explicated with analogies from our ability to comprehend longer stretches of time in one unchanging act. Our span of attention is limited. Nevertheless we can imagine how it could be expanded. For example, were we to become more and more familiar with *Hamlet*, we could successively hold in focus a line, the speech, the scene, the act, and then the whole play. If our visual span were larger, without losing sight of the detail, and if the Bayeaux Tapestry were arranged in a semicircle before us, and not in series of curves, we would be able to see all of it and its story in one glance. In one of his letters, Mozart wrote of being able, at the end of a period of inspiration and wholly mental composition, to hear in his imagination the new work in its entirety but not successively, although the parts have not yet been worked out in detail.[11] If we now subtract all our limitations then we would have, it is claimed, something very like God's eternal knowledge of temporal reality.

But would we? Followers of Bergson would claim that this is yet another example of the fatal spatialisation of time, as in Aquinas' example of the traveller. This analogy fails because the man on the hill also can see in one glance only what is in front of himself and not what is behind, and because the future for a created being with some power of self-determination is always partly open: the pilgrim could take a detour to look at something that has caught his eye or even give up and return home. So must all spatial analogies fail. For sight is our pre-eminent sense of simultaneity, synopsis, whereas hearing and touch are predominantly successive and inherently temporal. Whereas I can see a dozen distinct persons in a single glance, usually I hear only a cacophony if they all speak at once, and in the dark I could distinguish only two at a time by touch. As things are, I had to walk along the Bayeaux Tapestry and see its scenes only one or two at a time, and hence, going from left to right, I saw them in the temporal order of the Battle of Hastings which they retell. But, as just mentioned, were it suitably re-arranged and I had a much larger visual span, then I would be able to see it and its story all at once. Yet that would detemporalise not only my seeing of the tapestry but also the story itself into a series of static scenes. Even though I were to know *Hamlet* inside out and have the whole of it in mind from when the curtain first goes up to its final fall so that my experience of seeing it were to constitute one now, yet I would hear and see, in a focal now within it, each speech and each scene in turn. The world is series of concrete and changing events, and not an abstract and unchanging plan which could be grasped in one act without any before and after in it. Even if God were to have a fully detailed script or score prepared in advance, he would have to know what he and the world were doing in its concrete, temporal, and successive reality and also what he and it had already done and would do later. A plan may be unchanging, but either it is executed all at once or successively. Hence, in God's action and apprehension of a temporally successive series of events there must be a temporality, a genuine before and after and not merely a logical one, *à la* McTaggart—a changing focus that brings in turn each event from the background into the foreground, and similarly a succession of phases in God's activity in which each part of the plan is enacted in turn. A temporal world cannot be created, sustained, governed, and known in one wholly atemporal and undifferentiated act.[12]

Paul Helm, in his *Eternal God*, re-affirms the traditional doctrine that God is completely timeless and cannot have temporal relations with any reality distinct from himself.[13] His method is mostly negative in that he seeks to refute recent arguments in favour of some lesser or greater degree of temporality with respect to God. Undoubtedly, some of his targets are erroneous. But at least one of his counter-arguments is itself falla-cious—that concerning "indexicals," the terms which relate the speaker to the world and can be understood only by knowing who is speaking and when and where he is situated. Against arguments that God has to be contemporaneous with events to know what is happening *now*, he argues, firstly, that they would also require God to be spatial, that just as it would have to be January 19th for him to know that the kettle is boil-ing now, so too would he have to be on the Old Kent Road to know that it is boiling *there*.[14] But this analogy between time and space is false. In the first place, God is not located in the universe but it is compresent to him for he is its creator and sustainer. And, even for us, a sequence of events, such as the Battle of Hastings or a performance of *Hamlet*, can never happen all at once. But a set of spaces can be co-present as with Aquinas' man on the hill, a re-arranged Bayeaux Tapestry, or with the Earth as seen from the Moon. Not all indexicals are the same, as can also be seen in a later counter-argument by which Helm argues that if God could know only now precisely what is happening now, then he would have to be Paul Helm to understand statements such as "I am married" as made by Paul Helm.[15] The latter is obviously false but not at all like the former. For knowing what is happening *now* is a matter of direct percep-tion, even if at second hand—as when listening to a commentary on the radio of a sporting event. But propositions are vehicles of knowledge, not knowledge itself, and knowing that they are true can be very different from knowing what they about: I can know a lot about the current Prime Minister but in the primary sense I do not know him. The question is, "Can God know timelessly what is actual, what is happening *now*?" and not, "How can God timelessly know if propositions involving indexicals are true?" And the only way to know now what is happening *now* is to be in contemporaneous contact with it. A wholly timeless knowledge would be knowledge of a timeless world, and a wholly timeless action would be one that created a timeless world. But this necessary temporality in God's knowledge of what is temporal does not entail any change in God: *he* remains the same through the changes in the focal centre of his awareness, just as I remain the same when watching a play or listening to music or going about my daily routine.

Since a wholly atemporal knowledge of temporal reality is impossible, it follows that if God is to know exactly what will happen, then everything in a created world would have to be wholly within his control. Such a world could contain finite beings with powers of self-determination but they would have to be both wholly obedient to God of their own free will and would have to be given completely detailed instructions as to what to do. Not only would freedom, initiative, and spontaneity be redundant, but such a situation could not exist. For only finite persons can be given a script or score, and they have to be treated personally, at some point, and so be given freedom to disobey. Nor can anything be said exactly. Even modern playwrights and composers and the detailed codes of the Pharisees have had to leave scope for interpretation and initiative and also for exceptions in the case of the last. Hence, any world containing beings with any degree of self-determination must be partly outside God's control and so beyond his foreknowledge. It has often been thought that the assumption that divine foreknowledge is incompatible with human freedom could be refuted by arguing that God's knowledge, even of a temporal world, is wholly atemporal. That is not so even in the case of one entirely lacking centres of self-determination and even more false in respect of one containing them. Boethius and Aquinas were right in distinguishing the necessity or otherwise of an event from that of anyone's knowledge of it. Nevertheless, they missed the real issue which is one of divine control and finite self-determination. What finite beings determine for themselves cannot be foreseen, though estimates may be made of what they are likely to do. The future of a world containing them must have a greater or lesser degree of openness. In the vast but finite immensity of this universe, only a minuscule fraction of its course has been and will be open, if intelligent life is found only on Earth or also on only a few other planets. But to that extent, its course is partly beyond God's control and thence his foreknowledge. Yet this does not mean that God's knowledge is limited, nor even that he has freely limited it by creating beings with some power of self-determination. For a future that is still open is a "non-thing," and so too must be knowledge of it. Knowing it before it happens is a logical impossibility just like a perpetual-motion machine, and hence, it is no limit on God's knowledge.

Nevertheless, Ward and Hartshorne argue, God is thereby changing as accretions are made to his knowledge when logically unforeseeable events occur.[16] Yet, though it does follow that God's knowledge of such events increases with them, this does not entail that God's knowing, still less God's nature, changes. God's knowing remains free from gaps and error, for he necessarily knows all that can be known, and will necessarily know what will be knowable when it happens. And even I do not necessary change when I read the newspaper each morning. Even if I change my opinions about someone in the news, that may mean only that I now regard him, say, as dishonest instead of honest, while still abhorring dishonesty in public persons as before and not, say, becoming cynical about them.

4. Limits on God's Power

It is logically impossible for God to know the future decisions of any created beings with a power of self-determination, plus the results of those decisions. This, being a "non-thing," is not a limit upon his knowledge, and therefore it is not a limit upon his power. Other things alleged to be limits upon his power will also prove to be "non-things." The general error in these contentions is that God is treated as the greatest finite being rather than as the sole transfinite being and creator of everything else.

A long-standing challenge to the essential possibility of God's omnipotence is the Paradox of the Stone—that either God can create a stone which he cannot subsequently cause to rise or he cannot create such a stone; so, whichever is the case, there is one action which God cannot perform and, hence, cannot be omnipotent. Swinburne, who usefully summarises discussions of this paradox, proffers as his own solution that a person may be omnipotent at a certain time and therefore able to make himself no longer omnipotent, an ability which he may not choose to exercise, and thus he remains omnipotent.[17] Hence, God can make the unliftable stone but chooses not to and so remains omnipotent. But, would I be the world champion at chess merely because I never chose to play against opponents who can beat me? Qualified or conditional omnipotence is no omnipotence. Swinburne's successively refined definitions of omnipotence are curious in defining it in terms of what "a person" can do, as if more than one person, and any sort of person at that, could be omnipotent. It is obviously possible for a finite person to make something that he cannot lift. But in relation to God, the one necessary being and creator of all else, it is "a non-thing"—a juxtaposition of incompossible ideas just like a perpetual-motion machine. For as wholly created and not merely shaped by God, the stone would be and would remain totally under his control; it never could have any power against him.

Another alleged limit upon God's omnipotence is his inability to do what only certain sorts of person can do—only embodied persons can climb mountains, only married persons can get divorced. Swinburne's answer is that a person is "omnipotent at time *t* if and only if he is able to bring about any logically contingent [that is, merely possible] state of affairs after *t*, the description of which does not entail that he did not bring it about at *t*."[18] God's power, in the alleged respect, would therefore not be limited; for, God not being married or embodied now, it is logically impossible for him now to get divorced or climb a mountain, and also not to be able now to bring about in the future a logically possible state of affairs not caused by himself now. The last, we note, is an absolute "non-thing," a conjunction of wholly incompossible ideas, but the other actions are not wholly logically impossible in themselves. They are logically impossible only if certain prior conditions are not and cannot be fulfilled. The question then arises as to if it is unconditionally possible or impossible for God to bring about or fulfil those prior conditions. Consider the creation of organisms: logically they cannot live and grow by themselves because they require environments that will provide nutrients for them to ingest and metabolise. Hence, it is no limitation upon God's omnipotence that God has to create, beforehand or simultaneously, those environments in order to be able to create organisms adapted to them, for a living organism without its sustaining environment is a "non-thing." So, the real question is whether God can make himself into a finite and embodied person, and one who is either male or female and so eligible to marry and divorce if living in a society with those institutions. Swinburne's solution gives no answer to these questions because, as previously noted, it deals with persons in general and with not the absolutely unique, transfinite, and necessarily existing person that God is.

A third alleged limitation is that God cannot do anything which is evil. Swinburne allows that God does have the power to do evil, but also claims that God, being a perfectly free agent, will not act irrationally and for no reason, and so will not perform an action if he thinks he has an overriding reason not to perform it. Hence, Swinburne would prefer not to use "omnipotent," but in conformity with tradition continues to use it as already defined with the added proviso, "given that he does not believe that he has overriding reasons for refraining from bringing about" the contingent state of affairs in question.[19] In the abstract there does appear to be a case for saying something like this: that God may have powers which he will never exercise, so that logically he could wipe out the entire human race here and now, but morally he could never do so—or at least could never do so wantonly but only if any alternative were much worse. This takes us back to the theme of God's transcendence of freedom and necessity. Because God's existence and all his attributes are necessary, for him to will not to be any of them would be to will not to be all of them and so not to exist, and so to will the annihilation of everything else as well. Hence, these are "non-things," logical impossibilities. "Moral necessity becomes identical with logical or ontological necessity, when, what in isolation seems to be a power that God could have, such as to will not to be God or not to exist, is seen to be a "non-thing"—a set of logical incompossibilities when related to the whole of his nature.[20]

Yet it may not be as easy as it seems to decide what is and what is not logically or ontologically impossible for God. To return to a previous example: can God, who is immaterial, make himself a finite and embodied person, and so be able to climb mountains? In general, which prior conditions—all, some, or none—necessary for performing actions that logically can be performed only by certain types of finite person, can he fulfil? It would certainly be logically impossible for God to confine himself to being a finite person, embodied or wholly spiritual, for then he would to cease to be God, the one necessarily existing being on whom all else depends. But whether God could simultaneously adopt a finite form while remaining wholly himself, and whether this would be possible only if God were Two (or Three) in One and not simply One, are questions that perhaps cannot be answered *a priori*.

Another open question may be the extent of the power of created, self-responsible persons to set limits to God's power. To some extent God could, and perhaps does, deal with persons in sub-personal ways, such as by using the spontaneous workings of their minds to put ideas into their heads without their knowing it. But, at some point, persons have to be treated personally—to have their own free and fully conscious choice engaged. Otherwise their personhood would be destroyed and they would no longer exist, and there would only be some sub-personal residue, as is thought to be the case with "zombies." If they can continue indefinitely to defy him and, out of pride, refuse his aid or, out of despair, refuse to recognise that it is available (the two ultimate sins) even when starkly faced with the full consequences of their attitudes, then there will be limits to what God can do. Therefore, it seems unless there remains a spot deep within the finite person—a last enclave of good within himself that he can never eliminate and which, in one way or another, God can eventually reach—then God's power over created persons is limited and his intentions can be permanently frustrated. Yet, apart from this, to save a created person wholly against his will would still be a "non-thing," a meaningless combination of incompossible ideas, and hence no real limit upon God's power. On the contrary, it would be a real limit on his power if he could not create beings with wills of their own and who therefore would have the power defy him and, perhaps, to do so forever.[21]

Our consideration of these suggested limits upon God's omnipotence has shown that any plausibility they may have derives from neglect of God's necessary existence and nature and his transcendence of the tension between freedom and necessity. When properly related to God, the alleged limits prove to be no limits at all, for they turn out to be logical impossibilities and hence confusions on our part.

5. God's Creativity

Whereas Plato's Demiurge creates the world in the likeness of the Forms external to himself, Augustine completed the Neo-Platonic resolution of this dualism by bringing the Forms wholly into God as ideas in his mind. It was consequently assumed that God eternally holds within himself the ideas of all possible types of reality, and of their compossible combinations, just as he holds all logical and mathematical ideas and all their implications. But is this itself a coherent idea? It certainly raises again the question of whether an actual infinity is possible, for there is no foreseeable limit as to what sorts of thing may be possible, and so God would eternally conceive of each and all of them. The alternative conception is that God is creative in a more radical sense than previously assumed, and that he can create new possibilities (Forms, patterns) themselves and not only actual examples of them. Ward, already having argued that God can change, as well as be necessary and eternal, argues that this is a possible way of conceiving of God's knowledge of possible forms of existence. Ward appears not to offer any direct argument for concluding that God does create new possibilities themselves, except insofar as he conflates it with the creation of a world whose structure and course is not determined from the outset and forever, but in which new forms of being can emerge or supervene.[22] But the two are quite different, for the idea of creation leaves open how and when it is performed. Therefore, God could eternally conceive all the possibilities of finite existence and also actualise the ones he chooses simultaneously or sequentially. Contrariwise, if not having an eternal library of all possible blueprints, he could yet create everything simultaneously, as Christian tradition seems to assume about the heavenly world of angels in which there is neither birth nor death.

The question may be undecidable, by us if, on the one hand, it seems that the idea of an infinite library of blueprints is coherent and if, on the other, the creation of new possibilities themselves does not presuppose that God can change and thus would be finite. Ward rightly suggests that if God is radically creative, then it would not be the result of any imposed limitation. He alone would make possible whatever is possible, and he would enjoy the power of free creativity.[23] Indeed, one could argue by the *via eminentiae* that our power of "sub-creation," as Tolkein called it, for imagining forms of existence that do not exist (including truly individual persons and not just stock characters) points to an even greater power in God. The question would then turn on whether or not such creativity is really incompatible with the necessity of God's nature. Would the exercise of such a power bring about changes in God? The answer is the same as that given above in relation to additions to God's knowledge of finite events brought about by the decisions of created beings which can partly determine themselves: that additions to one's stock of knowledge do not entail changes in oneself, and cannot do so in the case of God.

Consequently, there appears to be nothing to be said against attributing radical creativity to God. Hence, if it can be attributed, it must be attributed. But contrary attributes cannot both be attributed. Therefore, if the idea of God's eternal possession of the ideas of all possibilities also seems coherent, then we must abstain from deciding between them until we can prove that one of them is incoherent. At present, I am inclined towards radical creativity at least for one reason: that it avoids the thought that God already possesses the unique ideas of all finite persons but allows only some to be actualised rather than co-creates the ideas of them when they themselves are conceived. I find something obnoxious in this idea but cannot quite say why.

6. Can God Suffer?

In Christian theology, a positive answer to that question has usually been taken to be the heresy of Patripassianism. I suspect that some of the reasoning behind the condemnation of the idea that God can suffer (and not simply the human nature of the Incarnate Word) resulted, yet again, from a lack of fully personal conceptions. All the terminology for the emotions implied being affected and passivity, and thus being subject to events and to being changed by them. Taken logically, that led to the

Hellenistic sage's cultivation of *apatheia*, a retreat from the world and into oneself in order not to be affected and upset by it. But as I have argued elsewhere, the proper terms are "receptivity" and "sensitivity" which imply activity as well.[24] And a mature person with a stable temperament is not *changed* by his emotional experiences but responds consistently to similar situations. Hence, compassion is called forth and manifested when the compassionate person encounters someone in distress: he *responds to* events, and is not *the creature of* them. To deny compassion of God is to limit him, to think of him as incapable of responding, and responding appropriately, to the suffering of his creatures.

But is Hartshorne right to infer that this reduces God's happiness?[25] It is interesting to find an authentically, but not exclusively Thomist theologian, Eric Mascall, stating that not only does God share intimately in our joys and sorrows, but he is infinitely more affected by them and our actions than are our fellow human beings. Yet God's own beatitude infinitely surpasses this and is neither increased nor decreased by it, so that "there is no incompatibility between the compassion and the impassibility of God."[26] How can this be? Surely, Mascall and the general tradition of Christian theology simply affirm two contradictory propositions—that God is emotionally affected by events in the world and that he isn't? But a little reflection upon some of our emotional experiences will show that this need not be so.

Max Scheler, in order to show that human life has four emotional levels—localised bodily sensations, feelings of the tone of the whole body, "psychical" emotions related to the interpersonal and cultural world, and the metaphysical or religious emotions of bliss and despair related to the whole of reality and to our destiny in it—draws our attention to the possibility of simultaneously feeling positive and negative emotions of similar types.[27] Thus, one can feel fit, healthy, and vigorous and yet also have a pain in one's foot; the former is felt on the second level of whole bodily tone and the latter on the first of localised sensations. Likewise, a saint may simultaneously experience the agonies of a painful death and yet joy (bliss) in the assurance of ultimate salvation into the presence of God. A central part of this deep joy, in contrast to negative emotions on lower levels, is the firm conviction that the objects of the former are permanent and that those of the latter are transient. Whether consciously recognised or not, it is a participation in the "joy of the Lord." And so, reversing the direction of thought we may distinguish within God, as Mascall does, the eternal joy of the intra-divine life—which is always all that it can ever be, and the transient sorrow at and with the evil and suffering in the world which can accompany, but not impair, the former. Again, this does not imply that God changes; the permanent joy and the transient sorrow are both expressions of the love that he is. The general conclusion to this chapter is that, although it is necessary to go a little beyond what classical theism has usually affirmed and to admit a temporal aspect into God's action in, knowledge of, and responses to the world, there is no warrant for regarding God as finite in any way or to any extent. Consequently, there is no need to reconsider our earlier arguments and conclusions. God exists necessarily and is necessarily and eternally what he is, and, *therefore,* he differentiates his activity in relation to a finite and temporal world precisely in remaining what he necessarily and eternally is.[28]

Notes

1. See E. Mascall, *He Who Is*, 103-4, 110, and the references there to D.M. MacKinnon and Abbot Chapman. Note also the refutation, 104-5, with quotations from Maritain, Gilson, and Sertillanges, of Leibniz' argument that God created this world because he knows it to be the best out of all the possible worlds: that for any world a better can always be imagined, simply because they are all finite and utterly un-self-sufficient.

2. On sufficient reasons as entailing a necessary world, see Ward, *Rational Theology*, 170f., 220. E.E. Harris and R. Swinburne also reject, but do not revise, the Principle of Sufficient Reason for similar reasons. Harris (*Atheism and Theism*, 8) argues that if God were logically necessary, then nothing would issue from him, for he would be *causa sui*, self-sufficient and not needing anything to augment himself (as does Ward, *Rational Theology*, 81) and concludes that God, as infinite, must include the world. Swinburne (*The Existence of God*, 79, 148) denies that there can be any "absolute" explanation of logically contingent phenomena for nothing logically contingent can be deduced from anything logically necessary and also asserts that God is "*the* ultimate brute fact" (267).

3. Ward, *Rational Theology*, 216-8.

4. See above, Ch. 4 §5.

5. For an explicit example of this, the "Cambridge" criterion of change, see P.T. Geach's, "What actually exists," *Proceedings of the Aristotlelian Society*, Suppl. Vol., 1968.

6. *Summa Theologica*, Ia. 6 2.

7. Ward (*Rational Theology*, 160-1, 168), Swinburne (*The Coherence of Theism*, 212-4), and Helm (*Eternal God*, 63, 87) refer to this principle but fail to follow it through.

8. A "personal" case for temporal finitude in God in relation to the world is ably set out by P. Bertocci in *The Person God Is,* Ch. XI; see also Ward, *Rational Theology*, Ch. 7.

9. Boethius, *The Consolation of Philosophy*, V, 4-6; Aquinas, *ST*, Ia 14 13.

10. *ST*, Ia 14 13.

11. Mentioned by A.E. Taylor, *Faith of A Moralist*, Vol. I, p. 427 (cf. 90-2), and quoted by Penrose (but in the context of wordless thought) *The Emperor's New Mind*, 547. Taylor (426-31) argues that, although there must be a *before* and *after* in

what God apprehends, there is none in his apprehension, but the latter cannot be wholly true as we shall now see.

12. Ward maintains, *Rational Theology*, 78ff, that Aquinas deduces from the necessity of God's existence and nature that he creates the world in one, timeless act and so it cannot really be contingent and temporal and cites ST, Ia. 19 6. But there Aquinas also distinguishes between God's antecedent will, e.g., that all men may be saved, and his consequent will, e.g., that some, incorrigible sinners, be condemned. As it stands, that leaves the future open to determination by the decisions of finite persons: see also ST Ia 19 8 and n. 9 above. The real problem for Aquinas is God's necessary knowledge of an open future.

13. *Eternal God*, 36-7, and 100-1 on foreknowledge. Despite his criticisms of many contemporary philosophers, Helm like Swinburne, is too close to some of them in four respects. He does not sufficiently distinguish propositions from what they are about. Hence he tends to identify knowing with the knowing of the truth of propositions and the modality of propositions with that of entities. And he keeps too much to the abstract and undifferentiated categories of formal logic to the neglect of those of personal existence.

14. ibid., 41-6.

15. ibid., 74-5.

16. Ward, *Rational Theology,* 152-4; Hartshorne, *Philosophers Speak of God,* 5.

17. *The Coherence of Theism*, 152-61.

18. ibid., 152.

19. ibid., 160.

20. Ward, *Rational Theology*, 121-8, rightly argues that omnipotence, as the power to do everything logically possible, can belong only to God as the one necessary being, and that anything that contradicts the nature of God is logically impossible although it may seem logically possible by itself, and that the problems of defining omnipotence, of which he gives other examples, arise when the necessity of God's existence and nature are denied or forgotten.

21. This raises the theological question of universalism. If, as Augustine held, love is ultimately irresistible, then all will be saved. That was not Augustine's final conclusion, for, constrained by what Scripture apparently teaches about the fact of persons who will be permanently excluded (i.e., exclude themselves) from the presence of God ("in Hell"), he rejected universalism, retained the ultimate irresistibility of love, and therefore and unfortunately opted for predestination. But if God is love, as Christianity holds, then either all will be saved or there are some who can persistently refuse his love, despite everything that God may do to get them to change their hearts.

22. *Rational Theology*, 154-6.

23. ibid.,154.

24. "Passivity and the rationality of emotion," *The Modern Schoolman*, Vol. LXVIII No. 4, May 1991, 321-30; "Governance by emotion," *Journal of the British Society for Phenomenology*, Vol. 22 No. 2, May 1991, 15-30.

25. *Philosophers Speak of God*, 511.

26. *He Who Is*, 111. See also, A.E. Taylor, *Faith of A Moralist*, Vol. II, 369-72.

27. *Formalism in Ethics*, 330ff.

28. Hartshorne systematises the changes that supposedly occur in God because of his reflection of events in the world, into a bi-polar conception of God: see the Appendix.

Epilogue:
Review and Prospect

The critical review of the traditional arguments for the existence of God resulted in a reformulation of them that stripped away the accretions and assumptions which rendered them ambiguous and so either tautologous or invalid. It therefore stands as the one valid form, not for the existence of God, but for instantiation of the modality of necessary being. That is, it proves that somehow, somewhere, something or some things necessarily exist—no less and also no more. Even if nothing more could have been proved about what that something may be, at least it would have proved that it could never be the case that nothing at all might exist and so would give us an incentive to look elsewhere for clues to the other attributes of that which necessarily exists.

Yet, it has proved possible to unfold and develop the idea of necessary being purely by thinking about it, and to demonstrate that it is one, possessing all its attributes necessarily, transfinite, expressing itself in all its attributes and all its acts in a self-differentiating and non-partitive unity, mental or spiritual, personal and the archetype of moral and rational existence, and (probably) having love as its essence. In other words, that it is God as conceived by classical theism. As for God's relation to any finite and merely possible entities, the only coherent conception of that is the relation of Creator and created, and any other would make both constituents in the one necessarily existing system or finite and merely possible. Against suggestions that nevertheless God must have some finite and merely possible attributes because of the existence of a finite world, it has been shown that they stem from thinking of him within sub-personal and merely abstract categories—although the classical conception does need to be modified by admitting a temporal but non-finitising focus in his cognition of any temporal reality, and perhaps also in allowing that he creates new possibilities of existence.

In arriving at these conclusions, we have thereby arrived at the true Absolute. For the one necessary being is that whose existence is self-explanatory. And, as personal, he is that which explains the existence of whatever merely possible beings may exist. They exist, and exist as merely possible and not necessary beings, because he freely wills their existence and does so because it is good that they exist—good but not compulsive. No other relationship between the necessary one and the merely possible many can explain the existence and preserve the integrity of each. As with any metaphysical and generally high-level explanation, this can be only an "explanation in principle" and not one from which we can draw any particular inferences as to what will happen and how it will happen. For the world, as the result of a creative and personal act, is merely possible in its existence, structure, and history. Therefore proximate explanations, in terms of prior causes, laws of nature, organic functions, and personal judgements and decisions are necessarily required for particular events and specific patterns within any created world.

But is there anything more that can be proved purely by thinking? I am not sure. The question of God's radical creativity has not been settled, and it may be possible for philosophical theology to say more about what God is and what all his attributes are manifestations or "accents"—namely, that all our personal powers and virtues are specifications of love. But that would require a fuller study than would be appropriate here and now. If it were done, I think that further inferences could be made about God's providential government of the universe and the destiny of finite persons: grace, "miracles" and life eternal in the presence of God. These would take the form of an "*a priori* probability." By that I do not mean something which is probably *a priori* but which we as yet do not know for certain to be *a priori* but something which is *a priori* probable. For it could be shown *a priori*, and not from induction from what has actually happened, to be more likely than not though not strictly necessary. This category of *a priori* probability is that of personal decision as motivated by the good, which, as we have seen, provides a sufficient reason but not a compulsive one. In any case, those further inferences have already been drawn.[1] And so, if not absolutely then at least practically, this is the end of our road.

Note

1.   See, in particular, A.E. Taylor, *Faith of A Moralist*, Vols. I & II. See also, from within an explicitly Christian context, J. Baillie, *And the Life Everlasting.* Taylor argues from the facts and aspirations of the moral life to their theological presuppositions, but, given the existence of God, then his inferences as to God's grace, initiative, the possibility of miracles, and eternal life (strictly speaking *aevum*) as the destiny of man, would still follow. Baillie rightly argues that, theologically,

arguments for the "natural" or "inherent" immortality of man are beside the point and that the real argument is from God's love. The former arguments (as by McTaggart) also err by implicitly regarding finite persons as necessary beings because it is thought that they have been shown to be indestructible.

Appendix:
Hartshorne's Dipolar Conception of God

Hartshorne consolidates his arguments for change, possibility, and finitude in God by distinguishing two poles in him: the abstract one of unity, necessity, and eternity; and the concrete one of plurality, possibility and temporality—a conception taken from the much more immanentist philosophy of A. N. Whitehead. As necessary and eternal, God yet needs to create a world of some sort or other to make the abstract pole concrete.

Hartshorne invokes a "Law of Polarity" according to which the ascription of a term also requires the ascription of its opposite, so that God (and everything else) is bi-polar.[1] But it has already been shown that knowledge and the virtues do not need their opposites but the reverse, and Hartshorne agrees that God has perfections—such as righteousness, wisdom, and power— which do not have negative poles.[2] That is, there is an asymmetrical polarity in which the positive term (e.g., knowledge) does not require its opposite (error) but the opposite term does require the former. The opposite is a polar term whereas the positive is not. Hence, there is no *law* of polarity but each term must be examined by and for itself.

Hartshorne himself employs the idea of an asymmetical relation of dependence in relation to God and the world. Whereas classical theism holds that God does not depend upon anything but any world must depend totally upon God, Hartshorne seeks to show that God does depend upon and must create *a* world but the world which is created, and what it consists of, depends wholly upon him. However, he argues that God's pole of unity, necessity, and eternity depends upon his contingent pole of plurality, possibility, and temporality for the former attributes are abstractions from and lesser forms of the latter.[3] In turn, that contingent pole depends upon the created world for it is constituted by God's reflection of the changes in it. This, he explicitly states, reverses the traditional evaluation of the former set of attributes as greater than the latter. Yet the actual consequence of this reasoning would be that God *wholly* depends upon the world that he is supposed to create. For the necessary pole, as merely abstract in itself, cannot exist without the contingent pole that is concrete, but it is concrete only because it reflects the changing world. In a logical sense, even if not in a temporal one, it is the world that must exist first so that God can be a concrete reality by reflecting it. The asymmetry therefore applies in the reverse direction.

In any case, his application of the alleged Law of Polarity to necessity and eternity, on the one hand, and possibility and temporality, on the other, is mistaken. For the former set are the full forms and the latter the lesser ones. Necessity is being able to exist and also not being able not to exist, whereas (mere) possibility is only the former and entails the liability of not existing at all. Likewise eternity is being all that one can be without loss, whereas temporality is serial existence and being liable to loss and gain. As regards unity, Hartshorne is somewhat ambiguous as to its two meanings: (a) unity versus plurality, or one among many, and (b) unity versus diversity or variety. He only mentions (a),[4] and of (b) he says, when arguing that there are good and bad versions of each pair, only that if the variety overbalances the unity the result is chaos and discord, and that if the unity overbalances the variety, there is monotony or triviality.[5] He does not explicitly show that they are polar but he seems, in respect of (b), to be thinking in terms of a whole and distinct parts that are polar, and not of the self-differentiating unity of the person that transcends any form of a whole and its parts and can express itself fully in each differentiation. As for (a) as an example of the Law of Polarity, ironically that would have a consequence which would undercut most of his argument, as it does that of Ward. Given that unity and plurality are polar, any one being would require the co-existence of others, and supremely so on the personal level, for persons are persons in relation. God, therefore, would be supremely one-with-equals such that, in contrast to polytheism, he would not be merely a one among equals or a chief among the rest. In contrast to monism, he wouldn't wholly absorb others into himself, but instead he would transcend the boundaries inherent among finite persons while also preserving individuality. In that case, God would be at least One in Two and Two in One, as we have shown. And that would provide the fullness of concrete being which Hartshorne, who never mentions Trinitarian theology, merely assumes to be supplied only by the finite world.

It is strange that Hartshorne, who did so much to defend the notion of necessary existence and the validity of Anselm's second ontological argument, should construct a conception of God in relation to the world which logically reduces God to a finite counterpart of the world and wholly dependent upon it, though supposed to create it.

Notes

1.   *Philosophers Speak of God*, 2.
2.   ibid., 9.
3.   ibid., 508-10. See also *A Natural Theology for Our Time*, 42, where Hartshorne states that the primordial and everlasting qualities of God alone would be an abstraction and not the concrete divine life.
4.   ibid., 508.
5.   ibid., 2-6.

Bibliography

Alexander, S. *Space, Time and Deity*, Vol. 2. London, 1927.

Allen, R.T., *Education of Autonomous Man*. Guildford: Ashgate, 1991.

——, *The Structure of Value*. Guildford: Ashgate, 1993.

——, *Transcendence and Immanence in the Philosophy of Michael Polanyi and Christian Theism*. Lewiston, NY: Edwin Mellen Press, 1992.

Anselm, St., *St Anslem: Basic Writings*, trans. S.N. Deane, 2nd ed. with "Introduction'" by Charles Hartshorne. La Salle, IL: Open Court Pub. Co., 1962.

Baillie, J., *And the Life Everlasting*. London: Oxford University Press, 1934.

Barnes, J., *The Ontological Argument*. London: Macmillan, 1972.

Bengtsson, J.O., *The Worldview of Personalism: Origins and Early Development*. Oxford: Oxford University Press, 2006.

Bertocci, P., *The Person God Is*. London: Allen and Unwin, 1970.

Blanshard, B., *Reason and Analysis*. London: Allen and Unwin, 1962.

Bosanquet, B., *The Psychology of the Moral Self*. London: Macmillan, 1897.

——, *The Principle of Individuality and Value*. London: Macmillan, 1912.

——, *The Value and Destiny of the Individual*. London: Macmillan, 1913.

——, *Science and Philosophy*. London: Allen & Unwin, 1927.

Bradley, F. H., *Ethical Studies*. Oxford: Clarendon Press, 2nd ed. 1927.

——, *Appearance and Reality*. Oxford: Clarendon Press, 2nd. ed. 1897.

Brightman, E.S., *The Problem of God*. Abingdon Press: NY, 1930.

——, *A Philosophy of Religion*. Prentice-Hall, 1940; Wesport, Conn: Greenwood Press, 1969.

Burnaby, J., *Amor Dei, A study of the religion of St Augustine*. London: Hodder & Stoughton, 1938.

Collingwood, R.G., *The Principles of History*, ed. Dray and van der Dussen. Oxford: Oxford University Press, 1999.

Cowburn, J., *Love and the Person*. London: Geoffrey Chapman, 1967.

Findlay, J.N., *The Ascent to the Absolute*. London: Allen and Unwin, 1972.

Hartshorne, C., *The Logic of Perfection*. La Salle, IL: Open Court, 1962.

——, "Introduction" to *St. Anselm: Basic Writings*. La Salle, IL: Open Court, 1962.

——, *A Natural Theology for Our Time*. La Salle, IL: Open Court, 1967

Hartshorne, C. and Reese, W., *Philosophers Speak of God*. Chicago: University of Chicago Press, 1953.

Harris, E.E., *The Foundations of Metaphysics in Science*. London: Allen and Unwin, 1965; Lanham, MD: University Press of America, 1983; Atlantic Highlands, NJ: Humanities Press, 1993.

——, *Atheism and Theism.* Tulane University Press, 1977; NJ: Humanities Press, 1993.

——, *The Restitution of Metaphysics.* Amherst, NY: Humanity Books, 2000.

Hegel, G.W.F., *The Logic of Hegel*, trans. W. Wallace. Oxford: Oxford University Press, 2nd ed. 1892.

Hick, J. & McGill, A.C., *The Many Faced Argument.* London: Macmillan, 1968.

Hume, D., *Dialogues on Natural Religion.* Harmondsworth: Penguin, 1990.

——, *Treatise of Human Nature.* 1739.

Inwagen, P. van, *Metaphysics.* Oxford: Oxford University Press, 1993.

Jaki, S., *The Road of Science and the Ways of God.* Edinburgh: Scottish Academic Press; and Chicago: Chicago University Press, 1978.

Jonas, H., *The Phenomenon of Life: Toward a Philosophical Biology.* New York: Harper and Row, 1963; new ed., New York: Dell, 1966; 2nd new ed., Chicago: University of Chicago Press, 1982.

Kant, I., *Critique of Pure Reason*, trans. N. Kemp Smith. London: Macmillan, 1933.

——, *Religion within the Bounds of Pure Reason Alone*, trans. Greene and Hudson. Harper, 1960.

Macmurray, J., *Persons in Relation.* London: Faber, 1961.

Macquarrie, J., *In Search of Deity.* London: SCM Press, 1984.

McTaggart, J.M.E., *The Nature of Existence.* Cambridge: Cambridge University Press, Vol. I 1921, Vol. II 1927.

Martin, G.M., *Does It Matter? The Unsustainable World of the Materialists.* Edinburgh: Floris Books, 2005.

Mascall, E., *He Who Is.* London: Longmans, Green, 1943.

——, *Existence and Analogy.* London: Darton, Longman and Todd, 1946.

Oppy, G., *Ontological Arguments and Beliefs in God.* Cambridge: Cambridge University Press, 1995.

Passmore, J.A., *Philosophical Reasoning.* London: Duckworth, 2nd ed. 1970.

Penrose, R., *The Emperor's New Mind.* Oxford: Oxford University Press, 1989.

Plantinga, A., *The Ontological Argument.* Garden City, NY: Doubleday, 1965.

Polanyi, M., *Personal Knowledge.* London: Routledge, 1958.

——, *The Tacit Dimension.* Garden City, NY: Doubleday, 1966.

——, *Society, Economics and Philosophy*, ed. R.T. Allen. New Brunswick, NJ: Transaction Publishers, 1997.

Radhakrishnan, S. & Moore, C. (eds), *A Source Book in Indian Philosophy.* Princeton, NJ: Princeton University Press, 1957.

Rist, J.M., *Plotinus: The Road to Reality.* Cambridge: Cambridge University Press, 1967.

Scheler, M. *Formalism in Ethics and the Non-Formal Ethics of Value,* trans. M. Frings and R.L.Funk. Evanston, IL: Northwestern UP, 1973. "Love and knowledge," in *Max Scheler. On Feeling, Knowing, and Valuing. Selected Writings*, trans. H.J. Bershady and P. Haley. Chicago: Chicago University Press, 1992.

——, *Man's Place in the Cosmos*, trans. H. Meyerhoff. Boston: Beacon Press, 1961.

——, *The Nature of Sympathy*, trans. P. Heath. London: Routledge, 1954.

Skinner, B.F., *Beyond Freedom and Dignity*. New York: Bantam Books, 1972.

Smuts, J., *Holism and Evolution*. London: Macmillan, 1926; reprinted Cape Town: N & S Press, 1987.

Sorley, W., *Moral Values and the Idea of God*. Cambridge: Cambridge University Press, 3rd ed. 1935.

Strawson, P., *Individuals*. London: Methuen, 1959.

Swinburne, R., *The Coherence of Theism*. Oxford: Clarendon Press, 1977; rev. ed. 1993.

——, *The Existence of God*. Oxford: Clarendon Press, 1979; 2nd ed. 2004.

Taylor, A.E., *The Faith of a Moralist*, 2 Vols. London: Macmillan, 1930.

Ward, K., *Rational Theology and the Creativity of God*. Oxford: Basil Blackwell, 1982.

Index

Absolute, the, vii, 15, 22, 47, 51, 65, 68, 83
Acosmism, 51-4, 61
Alexander, S., 54, 65
Allen, R.T., 30 n.4, n. 8, 48
Analogy, nature of, 26, 28-9, 58
Anselm, St, vii, 1-5, 6, 8
Aquinas, St Thomas, Thomism, 26, 29, 47, 71-3, 74, 80, 82, 89
Aristotle; Aristotelian, vii, 18, 27, 38, 46
Attributes: absolute and relative, 23; exclusive and non-exclusive, 21-3, 44
Augustine, St, 30, 49, 53, 78, 82
Averoës, 38
Avicenna, 38

Baillie, J., 84
Being: categories or modalities of, 11-12; impossible, 11; maximal, vii, 2-5, 7, 9, 11; necessary, 11-15, Chs 3 and 4; perfect, Ch. 1 passim; possible, 11-12. *See also*, Existence, God
Bergson, H., 66, 72
Bertocci, P., 81
Blanshard, B., 54, 55
Boethius, 71, 74
Bosanquet, B., 38
Bradley, F.H., 22, 48, 54, 65
Brahman, vii, 15, 22, 26, 47, 52-3, 54
Brightman, E., 66
Buddhism, 22
Burnaby, J., 49

Caird, E., 59
Chapman, Abbot, 81
Collingwood, R.G., 66
Consciousness: as impersonal, 37-40; self-consciousness, 40
Cowburn, J., 48
Creation, 59, 62-4, 70, 78-9

Cusa, Nicholas of, Cusanus, Cusanian thesis, 22, 48, 59, 62

Darwinism, Neo-Darwinism, 56
Deism, 63
Descartes, R., 3, 6, 8, 10, 34, 35
Determinism, 55-6
Dionysius (Pseudo), 48
Dualism: of mind and body, 33-6; of God and the world, 58-61; of necessary and merely possible existence, 58-9; of good and evil principles, 69

Emanation, 61-2
Eriugena, J.S., 48
Eternity, 26-8, 87-8
Evolution, 54, 56, 64, 65-6
Existence, logical and ideal, 31-2; mental, spiritual and physical, 32-7; modes and levels of, 58-9; as a predicate, 2-3; as univocal or analogous, 58-9. *See also* Being, Necessity, Possibility

Fichte, J., 38
Finitude and infinity, 20-4, 32, 40, 42-5, 57-8, 59-61, 78, Appendix. *See also*, God, as finite or infinite
Findlay, J.N., 10, 16, 47
Fletcher, J., 36
Flint, R., 2, 3, 6
Forms, Platonic, 21, 31, 32, 41

Gilson, E., 81
Gnosticism, 69
God, the one necessary being: as the Absolute, 83-4; arguments for the existence of, Chs 1 and 2; as having all attributes necessarily, 18-9, 84; causality of, 58, 59; and change, changes in, 26-8, 70-5, 79, 80, 87-8; choice and freedom of, 40-

95